*Our Breath is the
Whisper of Our
Ancestors' Defiance*

OTHER BOOKS BY EWUARE X. OSAYANDE

POETRY

An Afrikan Awakening

Caught at the Crossroads Without a Map

Blood Luxury

Whose America?

Black Phoenix Uprising

ESSAYS

Akoben: A Call To Action

So the Spoken Word Won't Be Broken

Misogyny and the Emcee: Sex, Race and Hip Hop

SPEECHES

Black Anti-Ballistic Missives: Against War, Against Racism

Commemorating King: Speeches Honoring the Civil Rights Movement

OUR BREATH IS THE WHISPER OF OUR ANCESTORS' DEFIANCE

The Poetry Anthology
1993-2023

EWUARE X. OSAYANDE

XOLA MEDIA

Library of Congress Cataloging-in-Publication Data

Osayande, Ewuare X., 1970–
Our breath is the whisper of our ancestors' defiance /
Ewuare X. Osayande. — 1st ed.
Poems.
ISBN: 979-8-9854925-2-1 (hardcover)
ISBN: 979-8-9854925-0-7 (paperback)
ISBN: 979-8-9854925-1-4 (digital)

Library of Congress Control Number: 2023916643

Cover Art: Yeabtsega Getachew

XOLA Media
Washington, DC

for Shango and Sowande

Contents

BLOOD LUXURY

WHOSE AMERICA?

BLACK PHOENIX UPRISING

NEW/UNCOLLECTED

Revolutionary Shaman:
Ewuare Osayande's Poetics of Black Liberation

Dr. Joyce A. Joyce

Ewuare Osayande's thirtieth-anniversary poetry anthology *Our Breath is the Whisper of Our Ancestors' Defiance* determinedly evokes Amiri Baraka's influence on the essence of Osayande's art as well as what Osayande accepts as his life's mission. The interrelationship between the two poets affirms one of reggae artist Bob Marley's frequently cited dicta: "Don't live for your presence to be noticed, but for your absence to be felt."[1] For thirty years, poet, political activist, professor, and cultural worker, Osayande has firmly grasped the intellectual, creative, committed, uncompromising, selfless, roiled baton bequeathed by Amiri Baraka's mentorship and by the indelible, comprehensive, communal, literary, educational, political, national, and international activities of the brave artists who fomented the Black Arts Movement.

Led by Baraka, Askia Touré, Sonia Sanchez, Larry Neal and a host of others, these writers permanently ruptured the influence of Euro-American aesthetics on African-American poetry. Though in some academic circles, the Black Arts Movement, frequently represented by the acronym BAM, has become a cliché for academic mobility and literary difference, the poems collected in Osayande's *Our Breath is the Whisper of Our Ancestors' Defiance* defy academic exploitation and their severance from the community and political foci that were the pulse of the movement. Wanting an art that reflected Black cultural rhythms and language, understanding

---

1.   See wooinfo.com/bob-marley-quotes.

that true self-consciousness would forbid exploitation and various manifestations of institutionalization, and believing that art should stimulate action that leads to change, Baraka clearly states the movement's agenda: "To create a true Afro American art. ... To create a mass art. ... To create a revolutionary art."[2]

The poems collected in this volume represent an unflinching commitment to the historical impact of the Black Arts Movement and, thus, at the same time, reveal the historical continuum of institutional racism and its interconnection to capitalism and imperialism. They merge as a patchwork quilt whose thematic fabric matches both Marcus Mosiah Garvey's and Malcolm X's comments on the importance of historical education. While Garvey informs us, "A people without knowledge of its history is like a tree without roots," Malcom X later informs, "History is a people's memory, and without memory man is demoted to the lower animals."[3] Osayande's poetic fabric includes as subject or commendation a minimum of twenty-five ancestors, ranging from Harriet Tubman, Nat Turner, and David Walker to W.E.B. Du Bois, Gwendolyn Brooks, Fannie Lou Hamer, and Paul Robeson to Charles Mingus, Ella Fitzgerald, and Duke Ellington, to Ossie Davis, James Brown, as well as African ancestors Patrice Lumumba and Fela Kuti.

---

2.   Amiri Baraka, "The Black Arts Movement," qtd. in *SOS-Calling All Black People: A Black Arts Movement Reader*, ed. John H. Bracey Jr., Sonia Sanchez, and James Smethurst (Amherst and Boston: University of Massachusetts Press, 2014), 17.

3.   Marcus Garvey, *The Philosophy and Opinions of Marcus Garvey*, ed. Amy Jacques Garvey (Majority Press, 1986); Malcolm X, "Founding Rally of the Organization of Afro-American Unity," Harlem, NY, June 28, 1964.

Just as we now see Baraka's contributions and those of his Black Arts comrades as literary and political compasses that enhanced the political nature of African-American poetry and instituted a vernacular and rhythms characteristic of Black culture, *Our Breath is the Whisper of Our Ancestors' Defiance* comes at a critical time in American culture when Black Studies is now weaponized by the conservative right not only to obstruct the education of Blacks, but also to block the influence Black literary, social, political, and cultural productions now have on Euro-American society. Integration has done far more than allow a coterie of Black academics to enter mainstream universities, it has also exposed K-12 and college students to Black contributions to American culture. The poems collected in this volume, aimed specifically at a Black audience and their allies, warn that Black contemporary productivity is an illusion that ironically distracts attention from the interconnection among racism, capitalism, and imperialism. Rather than addressing the collection chronologically, this exploration limns the interwoven thematic and linguistic threads together as they illuminate Osayande's commitment to a Black poetic art that uses African rituals, African historical figures and a gathering of African-American ancestors — Black history — to forge a prideful, self-aware, defiant, self-loving Black consciousnesses that lead to an envisioned reasoned change.

Many poems in the collection directly point to Baraka's influence and address why the poet writes. "a new day has come" and the previously unpublished "Why I Write" emerge as unavoidably poignant. The new day is the day the country voted for Barack Obama. The poet/persona in the poem (I do not fight these petty issues) "dressed . . . in the whip cracked flesh of Frederick Douglass/ put on Harriet Tubman's eyes/laced up Fannie Lou Hamer's feet" (lines 6-13). He took his mother's hands, and together they pulled the voting lever. Now among the ancestors, his mother whispered "a new day has come, son." Carrying within him the lessons and experiences of the ancestors who escaped from slavery and who fought selflessly for Black voting rights, the poet ends, "it has only just begun." "Why I Write," the second to the last poem in this volume, using the virtuoso enumerating, codified by Stephen Henderson's quintessential *Understanding the New Black Poetry*, aggressively includes many of the historical amoral, exploitative actions and crimes against the black body that deny Black humanity. The poet is a "vessel of flesh," "tormented" by the pain "of those lost, never to be found" and by those of us who are now "downpressed," as he alludes to Peter Tosh. Embodying the spirit of ancestors, Ewuare writes because he has no choice.

Always with focus on ancestors and mission, three other key poems dispersed within the collection have Amiri Baraka specifically as subject: "When a Poem Is Feared More than a Bomb," "Black Fire Blazing!," and "Lowcoup Too." Reading these three poems, we can deduce that Osayande has never been deluded about the physical, emotional, and financial sacrifices he makes because of the positions he takes regarding Baraka as a non-compromising Black artist. Baraka was blacklisted by universities and presses, following the publication of "Somebody Blew Up America," in which he writes,

> Who knew the World Trade Center was
> gonna get
> Bombed
> Who told 4000 Israeli workers at the Twin
> Towers

> to stay home that day
> Why did Sharon stay away?[4] (lines 154-58)

Personifying language to demonstrate the inanity inherent in an attack on words rather than a truth-finding dialogue aimed at capturing Baraka's intent, "When a Poem Is Feared More than a Bomb" addresses the hypocrisy and heinous abuse of human rights by a global powerful elite. "When speech is spurned/then burned at the stake" and "When eloquence is electrocuted," words become more dangerous than land mines (lines 18-40). Serving as the cultural worker, the teacher, and the shaman, Osayande ends "Black Fire Blazing!: for Amiri Baraka" with a stanza that matches the complexity of Baraka's poem:

> that owl exploding is you now
> in the tree of life
> eyes big as Baldwin's
> with Malcolm X-ray vision
> seeing thru they bulllllllllllllllllllllllllllll shit
> like Coltrane's horn blowing our minds
> forever who who-ing
> asking the questions where most fear to tread
> naw you aint dead   (lines 128-36)

In "Black Fire Blazing!," Baraka, the ancestor, whispers the need for courage into Osayande's poetic ear.

This courage also manifests in both theme (content), wordplay (African-American vernacular), and the interconnection between the two. Baraka and his fellow artists understood that if the

---

4.   Baraka, "Somebody Blew Up America," in *Somebody Blew Up America & Other Poems,* House of Nehesi Publishers (Philipsburg, St. Martin, 2003), 41-55.

Black masses were going to hear their meaning, they also had to feel it. If the poetry and theater were going to stimulate cognitive or any other kind of revolution that led to social, political, or psychical change, the Black masses—their audience—had to enfold themselves into a language that represented life as they experienced it. In this anniversary collection, Osayande includes "Lowcoup Too," Baraka's word to define the political nature of language in his poetry. Osayande demonstrates his understanding, as did Baraka certainly, that language represents the inculcation of a people's internal culture and reflects external influences. Therefore, a people's language mirrors that culture's worldview. In "Lowcoup Too," Osayande skillfully directs the readers' attention to those poems of Baraka's such as "Black Art" and "Lowcoup" in which Baraka unequivocally addresses how the distinctive language of Black culture mirrors an aggressive, creative, experiential resistance to European vernacular that fails to model the experiences of the Black masses. Like Baraka, Osayande continues to explain why he writes, this time calling attention to the relationship between what he says and the language he uses:

> Ours is a lingo of liberation
> always changing inflections and definitions
> anarchy articulations
> syllables laced with cyanide
> murdering you with murmurings under our
>   breath
> rebellious rhetoric
> communicating ideas that undermine your
>   authority (lines 49-55)

With the goals of liberation through inculcating Black self-determination and an intense awareness of how the historical wedding of systemic racism, capitalism, and imperialism determine the quality of Black lives, few means of economic deception, national catastrophes, or global corruption escape Osayande's poetic lens. This clever, humorous deployment of language characterizes poems, such as "Buck," whose title works on three levels, literally using the nomenclature for the dollar bill and directing the readers' attention to slave owners' use of the term for Black men and to the need for Blacks to "buck" the predatorial capitalistic system. Though the poet captures the exploitation, misuse of history, and misreporting of the planet's human, natural, and material resources throughout his oeuvre in poems such as "ANTHRAX ATTAK," "Bling, Bling," "A Raging Flood of Tears," "Whose America," and "Apocalypse Rot," "Dead Meat" fascinatingly highlights the peculiar commingling of humor and dread. Osayande coerces the reader to think critically about how society has become human stock for feeding the international monetary fund at the expense of our health. Full of puns and word play, the poem makes use of each word to lure attention to our relationship with what we eat, to its ill effects on our health, and thus to our exploitation by the food industry. The results of the glutenous, sugar-filled, fat-soaked, steroid-packaged food have consequences more dire than weight gain:

> if we are what we eat
> then we are diabetes on a stick
> cancer in a cone
> a stroke to go
> microwaveable bowls of irritable bowel
>   syndrome (lines 30-34)

Always hitting keystrokes that inform the masses of their vulnerability on a planet controlled by irresponsible greed, the poet sharpens an interconnection between capitalism and the need for Black self-consciousness. This focus in "Dead Meat" and in most poems throughout the collection heavily executes the stylistic qualities of repetition, parallelism, tonality, and allusion, all stylistic qualities of the West African oral performance. Two of the more dominant linguistic features in Osayande's work are repetition and parallelism. While repetition "gives a touch of beauty . . . to a piece. . . [it] also serves certain practical purposes in the overall organization of the oral performance." Parallelism "brings together in a balanced relationship ideas and images that may seem independent of one another. . . ."[5]

Taken as the reflection of a poet's consciousness and the political legacy bequeathed by African ancestors, this collection includes not only the deliberate for-profit "contamination" of our food, but also how the imperialistic greed for Africa and its resources undergirds global warming and heinous violence. "Blood for Oil" conjoins the interrelationship among imperialism, climate change, and violence, exposing that unbound industrialization and greed result in escalating global warming. Manifesting Osayande's stylistic diversity, this elegiac poem informs that Nigerian Ken Saro-Wiwa was jailed and hanged on "contrived charges" for fighting to protect the Ogoni land that capitalist-backed British royalty mined for crude oil. The "diseased" land ruined health and "cancer gr[e]w like grass."

Africa rests at the foundation of the Black Arts Movement. The arts are not African American; they are Black, the artistic

5.   Isidore Okpewho, *African Oral Literature: Backgrounds, Character, and Continuity*, Indiana University Press (Bloomington and Indianapolis, 1992), 71.

creations of artists, such as Baraka and Osayande, who consciously honor, but not romanticize their ancestral home and its culture. It is no accident that editors John H. Bracey, Jr., Sonia Sanchez, and James Smethurst place a chapter titled "Africa" at the center of their indispensable anthology *SOS-Calling All Black People: A Black Arts Movement Reader*. Similarly, poems that address African libations, politicians, slain leaders, musicians, and cultural artifacts appear in Osayande's canon from the publication of his first collection *An Afrikan Awakening* (1993) to the most recent *Black Phoenix Uprising* (2019).

From the highly selected poems discussed above, it is clear that *Our Breath is the Whisper of Our Ancestors' Defiance* is not a performative production. The poet does not exploit the high-profile violence that describes Black American lives; nor does he omit addressing the violence, responsible for the murder of Black men and the chicanery around Sandra Bland's death. The abominable violence against Blacks, social and political entrapments, and diverse cultural entrapments are ensconced in the context of poems that address language as a weapon; Black masculinity; Black male misogyny; some hip-hop artists as modern-day minstrels; the lack of accountability of so-called hip hop moguls; the intentional lack of quality for Black education; tributes to Ossie Davis, Paul Robeson, Langston Hughes, and others; the uncompromising sanctioning of President Baraka Obama; cultural appropriation; religious irrationality; tributes to Sonia Sanchez, Lucille Clifton, Gwendolyn Brooks, Barbara Lee as well as numerous other subjects.

Listed here in the order of their publication, the titles *An Afrikan Awakening* (1993), *Caught at the Crossroads Without a Map* (1999), *Blood Luxury* (2006), *Whose America?: New & Selected Poems* (2011), and *Black Phoenix Uprising* (2020) reveal a creative imagination in which the personal is always both communal and global. Coalescing into a verbal collage, the poems collected here illuminate the continued, never changing, but always evolving multi-faceted means by which greed and exploitation threaten Black survival. When reading any one of the texts, readers may find themselves thinking twice about the time period the poem addresses. All subjects feel contemporaneous. That which defines Osayande's craft is his steadfast recognition of the African spiritual tradition that molds his artistic, cultural, and political activism.

In the first line of "Verbal Libation," readers learn that the poet writes with the mission of an African shaman. "i am an urban shaman" signals a tradition in West African cultures in which shamans and griots embody the spiritual, historical, and cultural traditions of their people. While the shaman has the power of a diviner, the griot is the storyteller who carries the traditions of their people. As a revolutionary poet, Osayande simultaneously embodies both roles as he uses African and African-American history to conjure ancestors to provide strength, courage, and guidance. The poet advances the mission and the theoretical context of the Black Arts Movement by opening an accessible, intellectual, and political portal through which Blacks with scrutiny can change their reality. If readers identify or connect with the poet's vision for self-determination, self-respect, and self-defense, to repeat Baraka's words, they are fortunate to tap into such a "great source of power."[6]

A pictorial representation of power that is beautifully and impassionedly presented, *Black Phoenix Uprising*, as the title warns us, completely subverts the Euro-centric mythology of the phoenix that is reborn, rising from the ashes of its predecessor.

6.   Joyce A. Joyce, "Sonia Sanchez: The Breath/Breadth of the Ancestors" in *Ijala: Sonia Sanchez and the African Poetic Tradition* (Chicago: Third World Press, 1996), 18-19.

Presaging the defiance referenced in the title of this thirtieth-anniversary collection, the cover for *Black Phoenix Uprising* presents an image of a black bird spitting fire as it rises from the bodies of captured slaves in a ship. Reflecting the poet's thirty-year journey, *Our Breath is the Whisper of Our Ancestors' Defiance* functions as a djembe drum opening a portal—with African heroes, African martyrs, African cultural rituals, poems with ancestral figures, and allusions to a plethora of African-American politicians, poets, novelists, historians, blues and jazz singers, jazz and popular musicians, civil rights leaders, Palestinians, voting-rights activists, educators, political activists—which invites Black readers and their allies to move into the portal opening to follow the light shining for us to deploy defiantly the spiritual and political knowledge modeled for us so that we can teach generations how not to fall prey to the entrapments of systemic oppression. This compendium reassures those of us on the battlefield that we do not fight alone. With *Our Breath is the Whisper of Our Ancestors' Defiance*, Osayande proves to be the poetic scribe of this defiant generation. Once a student of the Black Arts Movement, now a leader, this epic tome is his Black testament, chronicling the movement of a people to a liberated future.

Dr. Joyce A. Joyce is Professor of English at Temple University in Philadelphia, PA, where she served as Chairperson of the Department of English Literatutre from 2012 to 2015 and Chairperson of African-American Studies from 1997 to 2001.

An Afrikan Awakening

1993

First Day in History Class

That first day of history class
in 2nd grade
was the first time
I saw Black people
my people
in a school book

And there they were
picking cotton
as though they growed up
right from the ground

No past before them there
bare
except for the rags
the sun bearing down on their backs
merciless as the white man
riding on horseback
with a rifle growing from his hand

And the book said
they were happy and well fed

I sat there
staring back at that page
my shame boiling to a rage

as I felt every eye in that room
bearing down on my back
the only Black kid in the class
seething

Whispering under my breath
"They lied."

What Happens to a Dream Still Deferred?

a reply to Langston Hughes' poem

tick
tick
tick
tick
tick
tick
tick

Rights

What's all this talk about rights?
Civil rights this
Human rights that
When the only right
Seems I got
Is the right to remain silent
And that ain't enough
To save my life.

The First Black Man

Malcolm X

was the first Black man
to speak to white men
without holding back

He didn't cut his tongue
on his words
before speaking

Or dress them up
in carefully articulated vowels
from the loose bowels of negro passivity

He never lied
or tried to cool the rage
burning in the back of his jaw

He never hemmed
or hawed
or try to beg them with the love of God

And when he spoke
he never shucked or jived
or bowed his head

Instead
he looked at them
dead
in the whites of their eyes
and said
"eye for an eye"

He was the first Black man

Caught at the Crossroads
Without a Map

1999

In the Be-ginning Wuz tha Word

I

(eye)

I

am

I AM
The WORD

I: the right here-&-now noun

AM: a state of be-ing

The WORD
I AM
heard
by those with ears to hear my sounds
profound

I AM   What I IS-IS
Isis
Reborn Word Resurrector
eye sight
vowels and consonants sense-making silly-bulls

I see
What cannot be seen w/o the 3rd I
((tri-vocal vision))

My voice be as old as the earth
The Nuk Pu Nuk
The I AM that I AM
ancient enunciations

The true trinity:
>God the Mother
>God the Father
>and God the Child

Universal utterance

The cosmos knows

Cuz I AM its mind

I wuz there in the be-
ginning

Time wouldn't be w/o me

The Creator
Oral instigator
Word Womb

I gave birth to it all

Spirit speech made flesh-and-bone

Bass

Tone

Treble

Verb-motion

Lyric-potion

Mouth Almighty

I gots da Power!
                        Mountain Mover
                        Earth Quaker
                        Tongue-Speaker

Two-Edge Sword Talker Life-Slicer
I'll cut ya in two
And make you face your own contradictions

I am
The Word

Wuz in the Be-
ginning

Sooooo old   sooooooo old Am I
So black and mysterious
My origins are unknown
So bad so bold
That when God said "Let there be light"
I flicked the switch

The Word
Want proof?

Then hush yo mouth chile

And listen up

Cause I AM the sho' nuff truth.

VERBAL LIBATION

urban shaman
at the crossroads
where dimensions converge
I purge my soul
by pouring these words into the universe

Calling out those ancestors present
the oral blast from the past
the priest's mask
conjurer calling
in eternal incantations
recounting history
with every name enunciated
lineage&legacy lingers in each breath

Tongues of fire act as candle light
for ancestors to see us through space&time
Verbal vodun
the egun-gun descends
and blesses the circle

Calling us to move
on the motion of our way
for we already have models
to formulate a future
forged from the visions
within our minds

We need relevant rituals
that'll challenge us to grow
and come to know the
WE in us
to fight for justice

Not habituals locked down in dogma
and irrelevant doctrines
trapped in archaic attitudes of monolithic African imaginations
Neo-negromanticism
where we were all kings and queens
when most of us were
artists, teachers, dancers, warriors, farmers,
healers, herders, skilled workers
who were sold out to euro-enslavers by our afro-rulers
for 40 oz of rum and cases of wine-coolers

We need contemporary cowrie shells
to tell us about our black selves
internal interrogations
lead to spiritual libations
pouring out past pain
unchaining our souls
cathartic release
letting go of those things that hold us back
in inferiority complexities
like looking in the mirror
at yourself for the very first time
and seeing someone new
that's the you within you
been buried under the debris

of fake, phony, frontin' facades
the mask that grins and lies
that distorts the truth
and contrives to hide
the vital force within you

How we gonna be free
when we've locked up ourselves
in the holes of our souls?

Before we can win the struggle
must first defeat the enemy within self
that demon that invaded our consciousness
got us questioning ourselves
gotta stop giving our power away
time to tighten up and think

We on the brink of a new millennium
of all people who've ever existed
we've been chosen to be alive at this very moment

You got to find out why
and realize our reason for being here

We can change our reality
we can change our reality
change our reality
we can change
      change our reality
      our reality can change
things don't have to be as they seem

Recognize that
we can stand strong as the pyramids
immovable as Mount Kilimanjaro
in the truth known
that we are powerful people
the blood of our ancestors
flows in our veins
when you call out their names
you're just calling out yourselves
cuz their life energy
now resides inside you
they are the reason we continue to breathe
so believe in your innate ability
to be the African you were sent here to be
actualize your full potent potential
put it into practice

Manifest your power in partnership
with the rest of us
so we all can achieve our destiny
as one community
healed, whole and free
a Revolutionary people
who never make peace with any form of slavery.

Lowcoup Too

for Amiri Baraka

We speak subversive speech
lowcoup
we done overthrew your language a long time ago
we diction dictators
who dominate the national dialogue
not what you hear on the news
but what is heard in the streets of America
where the masses are active and alive as our language

Slave legacy lingers
deep structure is a motherfucker
fucking up your
grammatical structure
sinful syntax
we transgress rules that stress
what is correct or incorrect
every time we open our mouths

We slow down the lingo
with our southern drawl
talking about y'all instead of you
about finning to instead of going to
say what needs to be said
this be our linguistic legacy

we be lying and signifying
why you think much of our discussion
consists of dissing and cussing?

Black boasting is burnt toasting
we don't play with what we say
venomous vernacular
we spit fire
got Molotov cocktails burning under our tongues
will blow a hole in your head
with our oral arsenals
we use words as weapons
battling on lyrical terrain where most fear to tread
because language is power
know that once the word is written on the page
it dies
all the books you've read
the words are dead
only the spoken remains alive
this is how culture thrives
like the people who speak it

we need speech to reach the masses
not those academic asses but the masses
who don't got no BA's, MBA's or PhD's
these are the people we communicate with
those who speak their first tongue at the workplace
where CEO's try to control how folk flow on the DL
paranoid professionals
wanna call for one language laws to be enforced
but no corporate dam can control how folk flow

Ours is a lingo of liberation
always changing inflections and definitions
anarchy articulations
syllables laced with cyanide
murdering you with murmurings under our breath
rebellious rhetoric
communicating ideas that undermine your authority

call it broken English all you want
but this here ain't English at all
this is Lowcoup
we done overthrew your language
when you cross these here borders
we rule the word

WHY YOU NEVER HEAR ABOUT UFO SIGHTINGS IN THE GHETTO

cuz we know who is abducting our people
those ain't no aliens hovering in black helicopters
chasing us down at night
with their heat sensory radar vision
like the predators they are

Snatching us up from the curb
to become subjects of secret government experiments
injecting us with viruses
just to see how we'll respond

The only X-Files we're worried about
are the real conspiracy papers
that reveal how they killed Malcolm and King
and how they intend to take us out next

No there ain't no unidentified flying objects in the ghetto
cause we know who they are
and they know we know too
though they will never tell that to you

For Those With Ears to Hear

STOP!

Catch the world as it spins on its axis
and ask yourself what do we need
then be it

Think outside the box
be the alternative to the alternative that ain't
that's controlled by the same corporate dams
that dictate the flow of the mainstream
be an authentic voice
an authentic image
not a regurgitation of some momentary market trend
be uncorruptible
no sellout
or souled out
a self that can't be misinterpreted
misconstrued or manipulated

Cuz being different ain't enough
if you don't dare to divest from forces
that exploit
that oppress
that dress up colonialism
and call it diversity
that turn difference into an exotic tonic
a drug to intoxicate our minds

and keep us transfixed
while they fabricate our past
and forecast our future

quit patterning yourself
after what you see
on MTV or BET
Honey, VIBE and The Source
are farces controlled by faces that don't look like us
these rags don't represent you
but the interest of the advertisers
who line their pages
who seek to make a profit
from your internalized oppression
resist the stereotypes they've manufactured for you
rather
be the prototype of what needs to be seen

Recognize
how our lives have been inverted
and be the revision
that will revert the repression
of our innate divinity
invent the reverse
and take us back to the future
and move us forward free

be the Sankofa bird
that truth that needs to be heard
be the Word
manifest in the flesh

Be that truth that bends but not breaks
the truth that is not narrow
but broad and above-board
not dogmatic but dynamic

Remember all the injustices
that your people went through
in their quest to be seen as human beings and
                Speak!
for all the times they were silenced
                Stand!
for all the times they were forced
to sit in the back
out of sight
out of their minds
                Love!
for all the times they were hated

it is their shed blood that enables you to be
walk with their memory
never forget
live with a profound humility
an informed sensitivity
to how the past impacts the present
and sets the path for the future
then step into tomorrow
anchored in the surety of knowing that
our truth is non-negotiable
is not for sale
or deal making in backdoor smoke-filled rooms
with politicians or corporate execs

who seek to turn our experience
into a marketing scheme
to achieve their American dream
that has the rest of us stuck
in a nonstop nightmare

Wake Us Up!

Conjure fury
and temperate with focus
and force them to face your justified rage
represent righteousness
be that truth
that in your face truth
that sho nuff truth
that proof that lies in the eyes
of all who suffer
and resist and rebel
and resist suffering
and rebel
who holler scream and yell
who give their oppressors hell
for all the torture they received

Tell it like it is
be that truth
speak that truth
say that
walk that truth
be truth set aflame
name your place

Know the
who
what
when
where
why
and
how

claim your time

Now!

Be blazing
blazing hot

Light up the spot
with your lives
so others can see a new way to be
out of the darkness of their dilemmas

Conjure the courage
Learn the skill
Empower the will
Seek serious solutions to our ills

better still …
BE The Revolution.

Doing Time

The downward spiral
caught in the vortex of a life with a question mark
the time
that keeps ticking
keeps ticking
that refuses to be paused in spite of the pain
there is no respite for we the weary
no time out to plan, to strategize
our way out of this mess
as the babies keep being born
begotten and forgotten
hearts growed colder
frostbitten by bitterness
each day looking grief in its grill
it's reflection seen on our faces
our lives been turned into feces
the waste of this place
as the slums expand
like the bloated bellies of starving children in Africa
our communities look more like third world countries
holed up in inner city cement huts
in a rut
punched in the gut by hitmen bureaucracies
whose ears have been deafened to our demands
by the sound of gold cufflinked hands
exchanging million-dollar deals
for the real estate

that is the land we live on
our get-out-the-ghetto desires have been blighted
our hopes are falling down around us
collapsing like our homes
under the weight of governmental neglect

Where our dreams get collected among the debris
that line the streets
where urban nomads wander up and down the block
huddle onto curbs
casting permanent shadows that is their souls
hollowed out like abandoned buildings
where they reside yet find no shelter
from the rain of oppression
the perpetual downpour

No accommodations they got
barely a cot and a pot to piss in
our lives are survival of the downpressed
instinct kicks in when all rational ends have been deaded
dilapidated determinations
accommodated dreams
our labor affords us no luxuries
lack the means to make our lives meaningful
just mean
just mean
just means that we are constantly conjuring up
some meager semblance of an existence
from the junkyard scraps
piled high in the industrial waste plants
of this juggernaut of bars and stars

Where we are locked down
in our own demise
handcuffed to our misery
and there ain't no escape
no escape
no getting free from this place
the whole planet is patrolled
and we are being caged right in our homes
where peace is a prayer that never gets answered
while the wealthiest go to sleep each night
never worrying over what new misery
will meet them tomorrow
but each minute we contemplate
consciously and unconsciously
the ever-present possibility of heartache
in existential anguish
our pain is perennial
needled into our skin like an infected tattoo

and time keeps on ticking
keeps on ticking
and ticking
and
Black life been a crime since Jamestown 1-6-1-9
and we still doing time
still doing time
still doing time.

Convenient Revolutionaries

we will speak out
as long as we won't get suspended

we will boycott
as long as it's not against our employer

we will struggle
as long as we won't get harassed

we will fight
as long as we won't get fired

we will protest
as long as we won't be imprisoned

we will resist
as long as it's convenient

Chad Discrimination

in the effort to accurately determine the intent of the voter,
the following chads will not be accepted in Florida recount:

Two or three corner chads
dangling chads
bloated chads
pregnant chads
chads on welfare
unemployed chads
homeless chads
disabled chads
Haitian chads
no hablo Ingles chads
ex-con chads
colored chads
homosexual chads
uninsured chads
any chad that falls below the poverty line

all the aforementioned chads
that appear on the ballot
will be rejected in the Florida recount.

This action has been taken
to ensure a fair and democratic presidential election

Signed: The United States Supreme Court

White-Out

*"This assumption that of all the hues of God,
whiteness alone is inherently and obviously
better than brownness or tan leads to curious acts …"*
W.E.B. DuBois

To be or not to be white
that is the question
or is it the quest to shun the rest of humanity
the manifest destiny
of those now classified as such
who used to be
English
German
French
or Dutch
and other assorted European ethnicities
but gave it up to become white
the absence of color
the absence of life

white-out

how does it feel to live in privileged skin?
in a world where whiteness is prized
and blackness despised
tell me
how does it feel to be the progeny of oppressors
slave master race

the disgrace of humanity
that you recast in your pale shadow
is being white all it's crackered up to be?
then why are so many of your own
trying desperately to be anything but
trying to burrow their way
into what they believe is black
which ain't nothing but the expression
of your own deviance
projected onto another people
to keep you thinking you cleaner
than you really is

these wiggers
neo white nigga lovers
or are they the ones in need of love?
guilt-ridden complex
crying about
"I'm not racist"
but on what basis?
thinking that just because you're not
a card-carrying member of the KKK
makes you an OK ofay

when did you hand in your carte blanche?
the white card that is your skin
never leave home without it
pale privilege
grants you access to everything
even things that don't belong to you
cause yours is a culture of conquerors

cultural piracy turned into private property
taking after that conman Columbus
crooked entire continents
culture of Elvis impersonators
who don't create
can't create
just steal and call it a discovery
in envy of what you despise
(what type of schizophrenia is that?)
vampire personalities
in order to stay alive
you must survive
on the lives and labor of others
blood luxury

would white-out the whole world
if you could
wonder bread reality
where everything is bleached and homogenized
stripped of all nourishment, meaning, life
and you just sit there with that blank stare
are you even aware of who you are?
Do you know?
What are you?
What did you do to become white?

Do you know?
What happened to your humanity?
Could it be that there is a hole
where perhaps there once was a soul?

CHRISTIAN CONTRADICTIONS

Ole' Time Religion

The religious right ain't
they wrong
mostly white
and quite racist.

Lowcoup for Christ's sake

If Jesus is color doesn't matter
then why was it changed
in the first place?

Preaching to the Choir

I once sat in a church and heard a preacher
condemning all homosexuals to eternal damnation
when it was clear that everybody in the congregation
came to hear the choir sang
and every soul knew
and didn't seem to care
that the director was queer

So what was the message here?

Jesus the Ghetto Bastard

If Mary were alive today and gave birth to Jesus
Christians wouldn't call her son savior
he'd be a ghetto bastard
born to another teenage single mother on welfare
with no place to go
because there would be no room
in their closed minds
to let them
inn.

Word(s)myth

Evil stole the d
From good
And made the devil.
The O in goo
Raised his first in protest
And became
god.

Afrocentricks

How is it that whites can get PhDs
in African Studies
While Black kids go to schools
without books
Thinking Timbuctoo
is a name brand shoe?

That's My Nigga

Way back in the day
when you heard someone say
"that's my nigga"
it wasn't coming from your homeboy
from around the way
                              but your slave master
and it wasn't a term of endearment
and he wasn't trying to be cool, hip
or nice

Instead
it was a word meant to convey
that you was
his
property
his
possession
his
slave
his
coon
his
you was   his
you was   his
that you was   his

nigger.

The Black Woman's Guide to Understanding Black Masculinity

When certain Black men say,
"Respect and protect the Black woman,"
What's often left unsaid is,
Respect, if she stays in check
But if she steps outta line
Then break her neck

Shaharazad Ali style.

Black Women are Black Too

The next time a Black man
Cries racism
When accused of violating a woman of the same hue
Will someone please remind him
That the Sistah he harassed
Is Black
Too

In Some Churches

Black women can fill up the pews
but can't preach in the pulpit

hmph!

Black women can usher in the aisles
but can't preach in the pulpit

welllll!

Black women can pray at the altar
but can't preach in the pulpit

Mmmmmm

Black women can cook in the kitchen
but can't preach in the pulpit

ya'll don't hear me

Black women can make the announcements
but can't preach in the pulpit

Can I get a witness?

Black women can teach Sunday school
Lord knows Black women teach Sunday school
but still can't preach in the pulpit

Wonder what would happen if Black women left
and took their tithes and offerings
along with them

and all God's people said
Amen and
      A women.

She Was There

when they came for me
they came for her too
on the slave ship
when I was chained in my own excrement
she was there too
surviving through the same shit
when I was finnin' to be sold
on the slave making block
she'd be there too
poked and prodded
like she was nothing but livestock

yea I was whipped
she was whipped too
stripped, hog-tied and beat
within an inch of her life

when I was working on the plantation
she was right there
picking pound for pound
from sun up to sundown

those were our children
they snatched out of her arms
children she bore
after working in the fields just the day before

yeah she was there

when I couldn't take anymore
and decided to run away
she said she'd been scheming herself
and was ready to chase after her own freedom too

mark my words, son
to this day I declare
whatever I gots coming to me
she deserves the same and more
cause there be things she'd been through
that I can't even begin to speak to

Meditation on Brother Malcolm

X

the symbolic embodiment
of all we are
and ever struggle to be
it's still unknown what will become of us
yet the debt remains unpaid
Malcolm
and you stood squarely
on your own two
shoulders back like a soldier

they knew you came to fight

you were the very being they feared in their whitemares
had worked for years
to ensure you would never be
but you came
taking aim at our enemy
your focus was getting tighter with each day
locking your sights at the precise place
where capitalism and white supremacy meet
it was either you or them
and they had the money and the guns
all you had was your word

and even when you left the Nation
and the man that helped hone you
your commitment could not be questioned

uncompromising with the lies
you were in pursuit of the greater truth
the proof that lies in the eyes
of every black child ever born here
and that pursuit caused you to break out of the boxes
placed around you by patriarchal hierarchies
you were beyond the times
for all time
moving at the speed of Light
The Truth
your cries cracked the sound barrier

we still trying to hear you Malcolm
still confounded by your complexity
wanting to repackage you
into boxes with neat little bow ties
labeling you according to our limited understanding
of all you were and were becoming

but then you said
make it plain
the only credential you came with was your sincerity
the only credential
that was ever necessary
by any means

BUCK

$@*%!

we are the

BUCK$

from which they make the change
we never see

primitive
      capitalism
           primitive

born from between our mamma's thighs

              spawned

from the jism of racism and sexism

                  class is colored!

we made over into money :: the loot exchanged for their luxury

nigga coonery issssssssssssssssss   slave currency

BLACK GOLD

mined from West Africans shores

CONGO COINS

exchanged before there were
dollar dollar bills y'all
we was owned by the dead presidents
we work for now

we was
the cash they captured
the scrilla they secured
the paper they pursued
the cheese they chased
the benjamins they were about
we was
their M-O-N-E-Why?
Because they robbed us of our lives

We were the capital in capitalism
the product in the production
of their bourgeois worldview
where being white
could have some social value

multinational trade
began with the triangular slave raid
rum for sum Africans for sum cotton for sum rum
from Europe to Africa to the Americas
transported all over the world
diasporing for dollars

before Wall Street was
we were the stocks traded
on markets called

AUCTION BLOCKS

no embargoes stopped our human cargo
slave ships stacked
our very blackness commercialized
how slavery was defined
rape as means to keep the supply in check
to meet the demand for more field hands
it was our blood that oiled their machinations

America in the black
is more than metaphor
it is irony sick and twisted

we have carried this economy
on our back sides since it was a colony
America's property
federal reserve negroes

black capital
the means by which they make their ends
real   estate
they held debates to estimate our worth
fractured our humanity into fractions
the original Cyborg
not science fiction
but political scientific fact

2/5 human
3/5 machine
constitutional acts took the axe to our identity
demeaned

business was very personal
our very persons

Massa's Cards
walking credit
with the signature of slave masters
branded into our skin
the bar code of bigotry

BUCK$

is what they called us

      money: the root of all evil

is what they did to us

they cha-chinged our lives away
like loose change

cashed us in
as down payment
on their new world

Capitalism put the cap on our capacity
to follow our own destiny

and survives on our willingness
to be what they made us into

BUCK$

to be the money they exchange
how they co-opt our culture
and change it into a commodity
for their entertainment

when our culture is our very existence
our very being
our very lives

BUCK$

Is that what we are?

BUCK$

Who we be?

BUCK$

How they see us?

Then let's be that and buck the system

BUCK

make them pay

BUCK

they owe us the very existence
of their economy
their very livelihood

BUCK THEM!

boycott them with our very beings
take our bodies back from them
buck the system
cash out of their accounts
stop being held in check

BOUNCE!

break out
steal ourselves from off the shelves
of the corporate marketplace
rob our culture back
Black

BUCK

divest
detest what they have done to us
and how we still suffer

we need sanctions
shut them down

we can shut this system down
shut 'em down
until they pay us back
for every dollar they've ever robbed from us

let them know
the buck stops here.

Blood Luxury

2006

A Defiant Grace

for Gwendolyn Brooks (1917-2000)

you, Harlem Renaissance child
you, Langston's lil sis
you, word-seamstress
created patchwork quilts
to bring comfort to the afflicted

god-mother of the Black Arts Movement
guided strident Black griots
to sharpen their (s)words
readying them to do battle
showing them by your example
that commitment to community
is what counts

you,
sparked by the Molotov cocktail spirit of the moment
took your Pulitzer and popularity
and walked defiantly
out the front door
of the publishing house
that owned your work
and railed a broadside against America
and named it
RIOT!

oh the accuracy of your words
the acute agony you articulated
the precise pain you penetrated
the loud love you lauded
the quiet contemplation you captured and shared

in you
was no need to boast in being Black
just be
just be Black
and the brilliance will fall down off your back
like the shimmer from stars shooting across midnight skies

just be Black
relate to what is good and resist what ain't
is what you left us

elegant as an Ella Fitzgerald ballad

you, dignity defined
a defiant grace
skin, black and smooth as onyx
like your words
lil black stones
hurled at the Goliath
that defies our God
and denies our godliness

stones taken from the brooks
that is you.

The Underground Railroad

the ground under our feet
was the tracks that led us to freedom

the ground under our feet
was the tracks that led us to freedom

ground under
ground under
ground railroad.

Moses got her heat on her side
her metal rod to part the waters wide
to steal away
steal away plantation's prisoners
moseying on down to the river
yes
ain't no turning back Black
this here be a one-way ticket
out of the most wicked system ever devised
just keep your eyes on the drinking gourd
and your mind stayed on the Lord

the Underground Railroad
carrying a precious load
black gold
our human souls
spirit-combustion

kept this train a-moving

this here Soul Train
was not a Don Cornelius syndicated lip-syncing production
this here train was black-black
black as Coltrane
engine screaming

        "bant
   baaaaaaaaaa
     aaaaaaaaaaaaaaaaaaaaa
  aaaaaaaaaaaaaaaaaaannn
        nnnnnnnnnnnnn"

moving to a rhythm of   "A Love Supreme"

doom doom   doom doom
doom doom   doom doom
doom doom   doom doom
doom doom   doom doom

with a Bessie Smith blues riff
belting out the smokestack
had hell hounds hot on our tracks
looking for familiar marks
on the barks of trees
ancient graffiti
aerosoled on the massa's mansion walls

The Underground
Nat Turner's hideaway

original fugitives
holding counsel with Ogun
machete machinations
creating our own briar patch
where the lash couldn't catch us

we was brer rabbit
outfoxing the fox on his plantation
singing songs and picking cotton
all the while plotting rebellion

is John Henry
born with a hammer in his hand
Black labor resisting them robber barons
laying down the rail
wailing like Fannie Lou
bout being sick and tired of being sick and tired
refusing to lose
seeking refuge from water hoses and billy clubs
seeking refuge for New World refugees
refused citizenry
Africa's dispersed and despised
a diaspora of outcasts and aliens
marooned on the island of invisibility
The Bermuda Triangular Slave Trade
paradise lost to pirates
with the skull and cross-bones
of the Arawak and the Carib
buried in their flag

The Underground
where James Brown found
the camelwalk-ing across the Sahara
and talked that talk
that only Fela Kuti could stand under
and dig his way out of the quicksand of colonialism
and resurrect the sound of black rage
from Negritude to rude boy attitude
the link between Marcus Garvey and Bob Marley
"there's a natural mystic blowing through the air,
if you listen carefully now you will hear"
Garvey's ghost in the whirlwind and the storm
whistling Africa's redemption is near

and over here
Jimi Hendrix is taking his ax to the flag
reappropriating national sounds and symbols
with guitar picks and tongue licks
the stars for the ones we followed in our midnight flights
the stripes for the whips that marked our backs like branches
the red for our blood shed
the white for our oppressors
and the blues
see the blues be our indigo-stained sorrow
hear him chopping down white cultural dominance
in 68 Olympic proportions
with the learned defiance
in Angela Davis' Black Power fist
that made the hit list
not Billboard's Top Ten
but the FBI's Most Wanted

The Underground as Panthers' lair
the Railroad,
how Assata escaped
is now hip hop running for its life
bleeding black feet frost-bitten
breakdancing in a winter wonderland broken
being hounded by vanilla-iced snowmen and frosted eminems
dreaming of a white Christmas
so they can unwrap rap
and go digging in the crates of our story
and sample our very souls
and bite our very being

The Underground is our culture crying out to be free
in double-entendre self-determinations
is the mystery never solved
how we still around
how we
morph
adapt
change
evolve
revolve
and revolt

we are the practice that precedes the theory
we are the fact pulsing that
we will never be satisfied with not being free

that this train won't stop
til we is free
til we is free
til we is see
getting to the North ain't far enough
til we arrive at that station marked Liberation

doom doom   doom doom
doom doom   doom doom

Next Stop: Reparations

Must be the Shoes

enter Spike Lee
playing a black man named Mars
like Marvin the Martian
homeboy from outer space
down to the sneakers on his feet
sneaking away from scrutiny
in a Nike commercial muttering it

must be the shoes
must be the shoes
must be the shoes

yessir bossing his way to fame
in 40 acres of prestige
with Warner Brothers logo branded into his mule's ass
flying on the heels of the world's favorite nigga
Space Jam
Air Jordan
double dribbling on black boys' hoop dreams
of being like Mike:
      NBA All-Star
      multinational product endorser
      imperialism's colored spokesperson
      smiling symbol on the TV screen
          selling you ish you really don't need

"and he's up up up and away …
this is incredible …
he's amazing …
Super!"
and other white liberal superlatives
of exotified glassy-eyed admiration

watch him on the instant replay
in slow motion
from behind the color line
as he defies gravity
and transcends his race
to become the most recognizable face on the planet and
"Damn that nig—uh,
I mean that boy
must have rockets in those shoes"

and Mars Blackman
is heard mumbling from behind the curtain

it must be the shoes
it must be the shoes
it must be the shoes

as the camera closes in on the sneakers on his feet
where his black shadow sits on the back as name brand
palming the brick
about to slam dunk
and smash in the faces of Southeast Asians
to cash in on a global sensation
and

Swoosh!
he nets a profit of 20 million a year
just for putting his silhouette in flight
on a pair of Nikes
that acts as black shield for CEO Phil the white knight
deflecting accusations of racism
as he jostles people of color in third world countries
and here

yeah it

must be the shoes
must be the shoes
must be the shoes

that got them paying multinational dues
slaving to the sewing machine rhythms
of Southeast Asian Blues

said it must be the shoes

as Nike tells us
"Just Do It"
and they do

just exploit
just oppress
just enslave
just do it to death

but in Indonesia
little brown boys don't wanna be like Mike
they hate Mike
and despise Nike
who own them and their families
paid slave wages
working for pennies in shops of sweat
in debt

their lives
like the laces they thread
tied in knots
never to come loose
they work far away
from the sounds of screaming fans
and the media glare
no reporters will be rushing them at the half
to get a sound-byte
for the 11:00 o'clock sports segment

for one
there are no time-outs there
no coaches but overseers
and no trainers to rub Bengay into sore muscles
or give them Gatorade after 18-hour work days

and two
there work is survival
not like here
where we pay to watch overpaid athletes play

and three
there are no retirement plans
or contracts
or agents representing these families who live in slums
where the sum value of their lives
is worth less than Shaq's Escalade

so you say the NBA is fantastic
but how can the revolution be basketball, KRS?
it seems knowledge ain't supreme
when the truth is that
we can't find justice on the ball court
cuz the arenas are run by corporations
that practice savage capitalism

they won't get called for traveling
into other countries and buying out governments
where labor is cheap
while poor kids here
will never get paid a livable wage
to make the very sneaks
they beg and borrow
to buy or steal
and why?
cause all wealth is theft
Mos Def
don't be confused
selling their shoes with our redemption songs
cuz when the whistle blows
there is only one winner
cuz our lives are always played under sudden death

and we don't get any free throws
cuz the refs are paid not to call the foul

yeah it

must be the shoes
must be the shoes
must be the shoes

cuz we the world over
who pays them dues
live them blues

continue to lose.

Patriotism Imported

And the Betsy Ross you honor
is now a Chinese woman
working 18 hour shifts in Shanghai
wiping the sweat from her face
with the fabric
that will become the flag you wave with pride

but how?

when you read the label and find
"Made in China"

why
your patriotism isn't even American made.

AND YOU WANNA WAVE THE FLAG

During WWII
German soldiers captured sat the Nazi asses in the front
while they're Black captors sat in the rear of the bus

and you wanna wave the flag
and honor soldiers never honored at home

they returned not to ticker tape parades
or presidential serenades
but the lynch mobs, burning crosses
"yessir bosses"
and their dignity robbed

we have fought in every war
for freedoms we have never experienced
the 1st to enlist the 1st to die

why am I so incensed, you ask?

On September 10th
I couldn't drive from Philly to New York
without being harassed

One Woman One Vote

for Congresswoman Barbara Lee

and when the planes crashed
the whole nation shook
like a California earthquake
Richter scale rage rippled from coast to coast
and when the smoke cleared
only one tree was left standing
you

rooted in your resolve
not swayed by the blind tide of revenge diatribes
of "somebody must pay"
taped to the back of some mad white man's Chevy van

and when you cast your vote
it was not lost in solitude
but was cast on behalf of we who believe too
and we all win because of you
420 to one
and the balance of justice
fell to your side
under the weight of your conviction

conscientious objector
conscious observer

you know that war can never bring the peace we seek
that just as the death penalty does not deter crime
war won't stop terrorism
you know
that peace without justice is oppression
camouflaged in the fatigues of social control

your moral compass
points due North to freedom
like the North Star did for Tubman
your roots planted deep in the River Jordan
she crossed for your namesake
Barbara

you say
honor the dead
not by killing more
but by stopping that which causes death
by honoring the sanctity of breath&bone
you defied those who worship gold, steel, and stone
they cannot understand your language
for all the words on their tongue
translate the violence

but you
in your silence
speak a word understood in every language
down through the ages

peace

I call you sister and savior
for you have rescued truth, restraint
and the people's dignity
from drowning in the gutter
of spit from the mouths of warmongers
who bask in the blood of humanity
for vanity

I see you
as you sing
this little light of mine
I'm gonna let it shine
one solitary flicker
struck by the match of your conviction
has lit the candle of our confidence
renewed for the millions
who call for no more war
holding on to the hands of Hiroshima's memory

shine on sister
shine on
to light us a pathway
home.

Strange Weather

We are the strange weather of autumn
the forecast is as fickle as the times

we feel the hurt
like the howling of the wind
the sadness in this season
the leaves fall like our tears
mourn for the loss of loved ones
the pain of this tortured existence
things haven't been well for some time
for most of us
we need not justify our actions
those who need to know
already understand

what matters
is that we love ourselves without apology
and that is a lot in itself
and at the same time
just the half
we still don't fully appreciate what that means
and so our pain multiplies
due to our willful ignorance at times
and our greed disguised

truth is a lonely road
horde nothing

not even people
the times will probably get worse
before they get any better
gotta dig the trenches deeper
no one knows which way the wind blows
or what it will bring

the days are growing darker
sooner
the dead walk without peace
winter is coming
our discontent has already arrived

this weather is as strange
as we are in this land
we were never made for this climate
why are we told hell is so hot
when the darkness is so cold
our Hades is an inferno of ice and snow
we've been frostbitten by bitterness

witness the signs of our mortality
etched in the earth
and as you store up food
again
store up love

start at home

and make no apology for that.

I Speak of Freedom

for Kofi Annan

African Atlas
carrying the weight
of 4.5 billion lives
worldwide
on your shoulders

but who carries you?

you stand
on the stool
carved from the roots of your family tree

you are their libation
their blood
poured in the name of colonization
now flows in your veins

are you an ambassador of peace
or a comprador for the powers that be?

cease the deceit
untie the knot of lies
unite with the masses
not the magistrates who represent
the dollar, the euro or the pound

let your voice resound like King
bring truth to the world stage
quoted on the front page of papers across the globe

disrobe the emperor
whose clothes are soaked with the blood of Baghdad

diplomacy should never be a handshake with death
this is no time for saviors or soldiers
peace is not a publicity campaign
but a process
meant to relieve the oppressed
from the burden of an unjust debt
thievery of a thousand years

who ruled the world
now runs the World Bank
do they sign your paycheck too?

whose pepper stew
brews in your belly?

in what direction do you pray?
toward the Vatican, Accra or DC?
God doesn't reside in bombs made by Lockheed Martin
but in the cries of children
in Iraq, North Korea, Cuba,
and Zimbabwe

how are we to trust
you are working on the world's behalf

when you confer with international killers
who break treaties
before the ink dries
just ask the Cherokee, the Lenape, or the Sioux

defy them on the principle your grandmother taught you
from a tongue as old as the earth

in the end
how you got where you are
doesn't change the fact that you are there
and that there are billions of faces
looking to you through the eyes of Nkrumah
with only the red dust of their determination
in their hands outstretched to you
with one demand:

I Speak of Freedom!

The title of this poem comes from an address of the same name given by Kwame Nkrumah in 1961. Nkrumah is known for leading the anti-colonial struggle that would lead to the development of Ghana. He was also Ghana's first president.

The Grateful Dead

you have no choice
there is no place for you to run
no refuge 'cept the afterlife

death wish is all that is left
after life's dreams
have been demolished
by bulldozers driven by soldiers
who believe you are scum

and no matter how many white Gentiles
holding up peace signs
come wearing bright orange vests
to protect them from what you face each day
you know placing daisies in the rubble
will not stop the rampage

and your remains will not be remembered
by the Americans that will play "Show and Tell" on tour
showing their battle scars and shell casings
sick souvenirs of their adventures in a real-life war zone
and they will pat themselves on the back
with praise for days on end
all the while you will be dead
and they will still expect you
to be grateful.

Anthrax Attax

"an unconfirmed report"

the air has been weaponized
scared to breathe
the slightest itch
or strange odor
got folk running to the CDC
for a report

gas masks make a mockery of the madness
ever try sleeping in one of those things?

Ted Koppel sits on Nightline
as the world topples
forgot to tell us that we wouldn't be in this mess
if America had signed the
Anti-Biological and Chemical Warfare Pact
way back in '72

as Americans sit eyes glued to the tube each night
unaware that
it's the airwaves that are infected
information's diseased
polluted with spores
produced by the STD of media whores
inhaled via the TV and print media
intoxicating you with hysteria
gotcha hallucinating

making you believe you are free and secure
when you ain't so sure

exposure to the tube
infrared ultra-violent rays that broad
cast a network
-ing to hook and reel us in
with the bait of bigotry

whipped into a frenzy
maneuvered into a position of fear
like a deer caught in the headlights
Americans rush to sign on the dotted line
giving up the only known hope for a cure
the bill of rights

a jingo ain't a commercial ditty
but history is a rerun situation comedy
brought to you by the makers of White House
instant democracy
no need for votes
just pour and stir

produces martial law
constitution suspension
rights on ice
government-sanctioned repression
the whole country is a concentration camp
fascism is back in fashion
McCarthy makes a comeback
gone retro

COINTELPRO reprise
the phantom of the Pentagon
Hoover haunts the halls of the FBI
I spy with my little eye
the rise of the 4th Reich

freedom is fiction
democracy a fantasy

record-breaking approval rating
the whole country's gone postal!

The US notion of advancement:
from the Bionic Man to the Bionic Army
$6 billion defense
and the White House shuts up the press
don't play that mess
better watch what you say and print
cause you're dissent could be your descent

if headlines were honest
they would read
"The Far Right Unites"
white supremacists partied when the towers fell
Christian and Muslim fundamentalists agree on the bottom-line
the Aryan Nation graduated in '89
from burning crosses to bombing abortion clinics
and subways with the Bubonic Plague

corporate drug dealers
push their products

on the corners of Wall Street
home test kits just in time for Christmas
Cipro becomes America's crack of choice

All Hail the Chief of the world's police
if Rodney King were a Third World country
this government would be the LAPD

but we must remain loyal
must remain loyal
must remain loyal
to Bush
in his pursuit of more oil
for the family dynasty
but will someone please explain to me
homeland security
for who?
for who?
when the first people here
had their homeland invaded
security for who?
here
lemme give you a klu

@ Ground Zero
the criminal plays hero
fiddling while New York City burns blaming the Muslims
like Nero blamed the Christians in Rome

@ Ground Zero
we are our people's only heroes
at the bottom's bottom
one with the soil
no stranger to toil or danger
laboring our lives away
born in war zones
bombed-out homes
from city blocks to cell blocks
our lives are perennially patrolled

@ Ground Zero
where we reside
at the bottom of the rubble
buried beneath charred
steel,
flesh,
stone,
blood,
concrete,
and bone
the stench of death floods the nostrils
holding on for dear life
the world's masses
enmeshed in a cacophony of mass confusion
crying out
DOWN HERE!
DOWN HERE!
but no one hears
us
no one hears

yet through all the sorrow
pain and tears
we still remain

there aren't enough of them
to destroy us all
we are the world's majority
and after the last bomb is dropped
we will still be here

chanting down your demise

No More Lies!
No More lies!

with the record of all the world's dead
with defiance in our fists
and their anger in our eyes.

WHEN A POEM IS FEARED MORE THAN A BOMB

for Amiri Baraka

When words
      just   words
are WARRED upon

When A, B, C's are   SEIZED

and held hostage

syllables assasSINated

lingo lambasted by gringos

When vowels&consonants are constantly
being SHOT out the airwaves

When sentences are sequestered

When honesty is placed
under house arrest

When jargon is JAILED

truth tortured

the facts have their assets frozen

When eloquence is
ELECTROCUTED

When speech is spurned
then BURNED at the stake

When they take Reason and call it Treason

When diction is discredited
common sense censored

When sanity is straight-jacketed by the insane

When they ban the use
of your BRAIN!

Then

Then

Then

you will realize
that lies rules this world
and our MINDS
are more dangerous
than all their BOMBS and land mines

combined.

ORIGINAL BORN

for Paul Robeson

he came   unchained

singing in the eye of the noose

no matter how twisted the knot
round his neck
he never choked back his words

vocal cords of steel
forged in the minds of Africans enslaved
the epitome of their will to be free

ORIGINAL BORN

they spit him out
blood sweat and tears
a talent and gift for every year under the whip

he carried their spirituals
from plantation fields to symphony halls
filled to capacity with the world's masses
dying to be freed
from similar masters

an ambassador of Blackness
the inversion of their madness
a renaissance in the flesh
running past white supremacy
in the 100 year dash

he was ahead of his time
for all times

for a time yet to be defined
a beauty too bold for certain eyes to behold
still

Jim Crowed
passport pick-pocketed by congressional hustlers
who called him communist
as if to curse him
cause he sought community with the world

they were scared of him
had to hush his mighty Black mouth
topple our ebony tower
our black fist before "Black Power"

they were scared of his vocal range
loud like a thunderclap
cracked the shackles of colonialism
his voice echoed the cry of 800 million worldwide

destined to win their freedom
the storm of his resiliency
kept Truman trembling under white sheets
peering out the White House window
into the midnight his skin

The Necessary Prerequisite

there is something to be said about sacrifice
about putting it all on the line
for the sake of a future
we may not see
and so when all the white kids were busy kissing toilets
after discovering how many kegs they could consume
or how many they could jam into a telephone booth

you were burning incense and midnight candles
contemplating action
that could cost you your education
or your life
and all the hopes placed on you
for being the first in your family
to go to college

and if you told them your plan
they told you that you need to be grateful
but you were in pursuit
of a greater need

they didn't see what you saw
or how you saw it
from the vantage point of visionaries
and so on that day
as you walked out onto the campus green
and marched to the president's office

with your list of demands
having only your blood determination
you weren't doing it for yourself
you were doing it for me

I know when you erected Black studies departments
out of sharecropper shacks stacked in the attic of your memory
you weren't motivated by the delusion of inclusion
for wanting our story told in between lies
you wanted the facts to act as rod of correction
you quickened the resurrection of dissent
not just to complain
but to change our society

the necessary prerequisite for changing the world

Supposed Rites

I was a suspect
long before they did a record check
arrested on false charges

an accusation was all it took
to put my life in suspension
between hell and fate

prison is a purgatory
a Black man's supposed rites
but I don't subscribe to slavery

I was profiled
hunted down like the game that never wins
caught
cuffed
wrists twisted into knots

all my belongings left on the roadside

in the back of a squad car
at the mercy of two white men
wielders of a power they don't respect
who never met my sons or know my mother
who wouldn't know me from another brother
and they showed me my mugshot
as if to get my approval

while they chained me to a chair
like a restless rottweiler
to question me
and so I sat there
quickly aware that I was more intelligent that them both
as they replied with a politeness
that was as plastic as their faces

telling me that it was all routine
the fingerprints
the handcuffs
the accusations
the dehumanization

playing the role of the good cop
but stop
what is a good cop?
is that like a good enslaver?
a good massa?
a good trader?

and had I not been able to make bail
(the Black tax for living under a systerm that ain't your own)
I would have been sent straight to the county jail

like my ancestors before me
I had to buy my freedom
but it is only as temporary as today

MATRICKS 1: BULLET TIME

Morpheus
Morpheus
Morpheus

Where are you
when we need you most?

too busy training
some white computer geek
while we get shot down in the street

Bang Bang Bang Bang Bang Bang Bang Bang Bang ...

imagine Amadou Diallo
dodging 41 bullets ...

Bang Bang Bang Bang Bang Bang Bang Bang Bang Bang
Bang Bang Bang Bang Bang Bang Bang Bang Bang Bang
Bang Bang Bang Bang Bang Bang Bang Bang Bang Bang
Bang Bang Bang Bang Bang Bang Bang Bang Bang Bang Bang

we
are as Neo
as neo-colonialism.

When We Will Forgive Trent Lott

the hood has been pulled off
another racist been exposed
hosed down in the bile
of his own vile contempt
for social progress

but God bless

he now claims
he's seen the light
the error of his ways
on his way to the press conference
to ask us for our forgiveness

it was a slip of the tongue
you say
a slip like a snake's lisp
your very presence is poisonous
is violence expressed
in legislative collar and tie

yr breath reeks of death
drink cocktails mixed with kerosene
firing breathing Grand Dragon

Southern Black churches mysteriously burn
when you come to town
you say you're gonna change yr racist ways
throw a few votes across the tracks

honorary provost of Bob Jones University
yr body will play host
to Strom Thurmond's ghost
once he's finally deceased

how many more Black bodies have yet to be found
at the bottom of the Mississippi?

what would Fannie Lou
have to say about you?

congressional aide to that Dixiecrat Bill Colmer that
refused her a seat at the Democratic Convention
back in '64

what role did you play
in making sure
Medgar Ever's murderers faced
an all-white jury?

why should we believe your story?

poverty pimp supreme
you sit behind your desk and daydream
of whips and chains
plantation fantasies

you and your constituents
still haven't forgiven Lee
for surrendering the Civil War

race whore
from the state
that didn't outlaw slavery until 1985

what was that,
an oversight?

the same reason why a confederate flag
still flies atop Mississippi's state house
is that an oversight too?

so you want to know
when we will forgive you

maybe it'll be after you reveal the names
of all the jack-asses and ivory tusks
that secretly hold your views too

or maybe we'll forgive you
after you've raised millions for Black farmers
a dollar for every cent you raised
for the Conservative Citizens Council
the group whose predecessor
funded the white terrorists
that bombed the Freedom Riders' bus

or maybe it'll be
after you've served time in the county jail
a year for every year you voted against King's holiday
and while there
we'll watch you beat yourself black&blue
a lick for every time the nightsticks hit Fannie Lou Hamer
leaving her crippled and blind in one eye

consider it a spiritual exercise
to purify you of any future evil intent

and when you fall asleep
you'll have an organ removed
for all the Black women sterilized in your state
without their consent
and when you awake and realize
what you lack in your insides
you'll be informed that all the replacement donors
are Black
now what would you say to that?

maybe we'll forgive you
when the klan has been banned
and all its members have been detained and deported
back to their ancestral homelands
or after we watch you burn Mississippi's confederate flag
as you recite from memory
King's "I Have a Dream" speech
then go to every church in your region
and preach a sermon on the evils of segregation

or maybe it'll be
after you show up to vote
only to be told that you'll have a pass a poll exam
the first question being
"How many bubbles are in a bar soap?"

maybe we'll say,
Lott, its all okay
the day your appointed president
signs into law the African American Reparations Act
that you will publicly support and work hard to pass
then hold his hands and sing
"Free At Last"

and if you complain that this is unreasonable
that we're being unfair
that we are mongers of hate
we'll simply remind you of what you said in '81
in a Supreme Court brief, that
"race discrimination doesn't always violate public policy"

maybe then
we will forgive Trent Lott
but then again
maybe not.

HOME

our homes were broken
on the auction block
when Baba and Iya had their child snatched
from their arms
her scent lingering in their embrace
their faces exploding in an ocean of tears
in silence

our families were never meant to function

but our freedom's eve
we weaved quilts
from the artifacts of our memory
and made a road map to tomorrow

on that day
we walked defiantly out of massa's gates
with only our faith as companion

the only thing that our mind
was finding kin and kind
with feet on fire
we walked for worlds
held our dignity close
right next to our emancipation papers
tucked between the whip marks
on our back

we saved our tears
for those we knew would
cup them in their palms
and promised protection
from the haints and horrors to come

we carry this history in our hearts
in our songs
in old postcards
in pictures that sit on the ledge of our legacy
with glasses of water
strange faces that look like our own
we carry this history in our memory

it matters not what those think
who drink from fountains
that did not welcome our thirst

what matters is that we re member
continue putting ourselves back
to get her
what happened to us is beyond travesty
is the evil that still goes down around town

we resist this
by replacing those who would be snatched
by seeing ourselves in their faces
by telling them "I love you" for no reason
by planting seeds for tomorrow's vineyard
to reap a harvest called home.

A Face of Flint

for Malcolm X

there is madness in the atmosphere
thick as the pollution
rotting the air

the world still needs you Malcolm
scared to look into the eyes of your analysis
uncompromising is uncommon these days

and after the towers fell
and Muslims were catching hell
your words were not raised

on whose terms do we live?

how do we learn to

see with new eyes
hear with new ears
speak with new tongues
feel with new hearts
?

I miss you
like I miss my father

though I never met you
I have dined at the table of your wisdom
I have driven miles listening to your chats
I step to the cadence of your clarity
measure my growth
along the rule of your development

I walk with the frustration of Walker
the page soaked with tears
for those willing to accept the chain

too many young bloods
exist in the shadow of your former self
trying to claim the manhood of a slave
dancing between cellblocks
spit bars that keep them on lockdown
incarcerated logic

the chickens keep coming home to roost

those two-legged dogs who
sniffed your tracks
hounded your footsteps
from Cairo to Paris
and barred you at the gate
are now commonplace occurrences for us of color

but you had a face of flint
chipping away at the plymouth rock
that landed on us

we need new direction
leaders with big titles
more eager for popularity than the people
no accountability to the grassroots
we are being choked by the weeds
of our unwillingness to take risks

love is a luxury
lost on the old and the young
hearts apathetic and cynical
diseased arteries of the spirit

we are lost
and too damn stubborn to ask for directions

all the while your spirit
stands behind the podium at the Audubon
pointing forward to freedom

Identity Theft

they say
imitation is the greatest form of flattery
but I'm not impressed
by those who dress up as the Other
in their attempt to discover
themselves

whiteness is the exclusive club
we Blacks will never get let in
but somehow we supposed to welcome
those who are the beneficiaries of our oppression
dressing up in our darkness

where is the court that would charge them with
identity theft?

this is grand larceny

invaders from outer race
culture raiders
evaders of justice
body snatchers
biting Blackness
aliens in pale skin
invading spaces that are not their own

like the Borg in Star Trek
swallowing whole peoples

cultural germs
white worms
infecting viruses
setting up comfort zones in my home

but no matter how much Blackness you ingest
you can't snatch spirit

the ghost in the machine
the spook in the jukebox
can't get got by mere cultural mocking
no matter how shocking
cause
no matter   how long your matted hair/not-locks grow
or how tight your flow
or how many versions of the electric slide or the bump
you know
or how high you can jump
or how long you can hold a note
or how many Black authors you can quote
or how many cowrie shells you rock round your neck
or how fast you can run

or how dark you turn your skin by baking it under the sun
or how fluently you can speak Swahili
or how many times you complement me

you will never know
what it means to be Black

no matter how many trips you make to
Africa or Jamaica or Brazil or India
or any other where Black folk live
you'll never be
anyone other than your white skinned privileged self

appreciation is one thing
but appropriation is what you bring
every time you try to sing
and say that you down with the Brown

Blackfolks can't have shit
literally
eventually
you'll see some white folks running up our ass
trying to confiscate our excrement

to rebel against the static whiteness
the blank slate dry and caustic
the caucasian chalk stick
on the global blackboard

what is it
you can say you own
at the end of yourself
that wasn't taken by force?
of course
you've been trained by the best

what makes what you do
any different than what Columbus did?

imagine him
stealing gold from the Caribs
and raping their daughters
all the while talking bout how
he just love himself some Carib culture

you need to stop
pause
get behind your
"well see it's because"
and reflect on why being white
has become so transient and trite
but what is true
is that you
ain't challenging your racism
when you cross the tracks
and enter into that dark taboo

no cops will harass you
you won't be followed in department stores
surveillance cams won't be cramming your personal space

so wigger please
give your tired ass response a rest
cause
our culture is our way of life
is our survival and thrival
in a world hostile to our very being

it is not mere cloak
or costume
or tune
or dance
or trance
it is our very existence

you dress up in the vestiges of our darkness
only to take it off when convenient
when it gets too real
when the nightstick hits your head
and wakes you up to our reality

like that white guy who tried to discover
what it means to be Black
only to find that he couldn't last a year in our skin
couldn't walk a mile in our shoes

we the ones been bruised
not you
get a clue

see
soul is more than a song
it's a long long history
you have to live to understand

rather than trying to transcend your whiteness
trace the history of your own race
go find yourself
that pre-white reality

if it can be found
and if it can't
then
go create your own

but whatever you do
leave our shit alone

99 Problems and Jay-Z is Just One

a poem of accountability

because of all the rapes
the bruises hid behind makeup or sunglasses
when sisters ain't nothing but tits and asses
for all the lashes
and the cashes exchanged

for enduring through the attacks
on their character
on their very person

for being considered just a booty
and the calls made to the police
for domestic violence
and why women are scared to testify
so they lie through busted teeth
for all the blood spilled

because of Nelly's "Tip Drill"

because women are killed for getting pregnant
by the men who impregnated them

because of all the Black women forced to wet nurse white babies
while their own children starved

because white women are the only ones this society respects
then blame Black men for imaginary crimes
for the Scottsboro Boys
for the lies that led to lynchings

for all the girlfriends lovers and wives
who sit in prison for defending themselves

because of Bush's attack on Roe v. Wade
because abortion clinics are bombed

for Jefferson raping his slave
and Americans calling that an act of love

because John Wayne called Native American women squaw
because of men who think they are above the law

because Snoop Dogg walked onto the stage
with women and dog chains

because you can't go to college
and take a course in fighting oppression

for all the women Biggie beat down
for why his murderers have yet to be found

because of Hugh Hefner and Howard Stern

because Charles Stewart killed his pregnant wife
and blamed it on a Black man

for all the girls missing and will turn up dead
for their sisters who are scared to go to bed

for all the women forced to sell their bodies just to survive

because women still make less than men

because ministers still preach that women should
obey their husbands
and counsel battered wives to stay with their abusers

because the Southern Baptist church banned
the ordination of women

because black youth know more about Foxy Brown
than Angela Davis

because of stereotypes
like Aunt Jemima and Sapphire

for those that blame Eve
and believe that women are made from a man's rib cage

because Sarah Baartman was kidnapped, stripped and caged
and people paid to see her at the World's Fair

because if men had to give birth
we'd all have universal healthcare

for all the unreported acts of incest

because little black boys wanna grow up to be pimps

because no means no
no matter how far she goes

because sex has become synonymous with violence
because love does not hurt
because of Nelly's Pimp Juice
because little black girls are called shorties and hotties

until women can walk the streets without being harassed

because R. Kelly videotaped himself pissing on Black girls
and the culture defended him

because of all the men that screamed on Alice Walker
for airing our dirty laundry in The Color Purple
because we have dirty laundry
until domestic workers earn a livable wage
for those women fighting to keep their family under one roof
because after all this
some of y'all will still want more proof

because I am not exempt for writing this
because I refuse to rest until this madness ends
because sexism is as real as racism

and the personal is political
the personal is political
the political is personal

BLING-BLING

around the block from Brooklyn
is Kabala in Sierra Leone
home of the diamonds
rocked in rap videos by the very Blacks
whose ancestors started the Middle Passage rhythm
that would become hip hop
but stop!
Pan African vision been lost
blinded by

the bling bling

the glimmer
the shimmer
the shine
the great white light
but is the price right
when the cost is our very souls on ice

hip hop's paradox

locked in the cell of selling ourselves
as Black
but what gets passed off as that
is a bluff
sold back to us
by those who count their investments

on fingers dipped in our blood

while rap impresarios
mined from ghettoes
serve culture on platinum platters to massa
emcees who can't see
beyond the shine of their diamond-studded teeth
spray lyrical phlegm
like pissin in the dark
keep missing the mark
going on and on
to the break 'a dawn
about murder money and mayhem

minstrels on the world stage
shot live
from satellite beams
to TV screens all over the globe

but there in the heart of the earth
red core
rivers run in blood like veins
no Jas rule
but real gangsters

here death is not glamorized
in movie soundtracks by
self-made orphans
after sacrificing their parents
on the altar of diamond warlords
who proffer themselves as gods

and grant their juvenile subjects
the benefits of a slow death

gassing up their bodies in the midst of an
African inferno
inhale cocaine through laced blunts
til their eyes
shot in blood
become their vision

to them
bling bling
is not a fashion statement
but a statement to how greed
bring brings
misery to so many

enslaved to America's fascination with shiny rocks

raw and uncut
like the stones
they dive into deep waters searching for
hidden treasure
must grow gills from the sheer will to not drown

and if they come back with nothing but their heartbeats
their punishment is dismemberment
when asked short sleeve or long
they're not having shirts tailored to fit
but given the choice between life or limb
as the hatchet hovers overhead

while your favorite emcee
decides how much he'll spend on
bling bling

tell me
what does Jay-Z have to say
to an African amputee
about a hard knock life
while he rocks the ice
they get sliced
for mining a business they don't own?

hands severed
but "diamonds are forever"
how clever
ad campaigns by DeBeers
meant to cover the truth

been bamboozled by the
bling bling
worthless rocks
hoodwinked into thinking these hunks of stone
are precious
which in turn keeps them
omnipotent as Oppenheimer's lust
ground black bones to dust
making a killing
King Leopold's ghost rocks the Stock Exchange
in Antwerp in Belgium
home of the soldiers who shot Lumumba

there diamonds are weighed on scales to determine their value
the severed hands of African children serve as counterweight

how do you calculate the loss of African lives
in carats?
our hearts have grown as cold
as the ice we rock
we are severed from our homeland
separated by more than sea
when we fail to see
our hand in keeping our kin in slavery
while we stand on the auction block
willingly

with our culture in our hands
and our bodies on display
the neon sign above our head reads
"Slave Lotto"
50 Cent
or a half a buck to play
which is to say
that we are
chained to the desire
to get rich
or die trying
and we are
dying
a slow asphyxiation of our souls
and the whole world watches in utter glee
as we swing from the money tree
our faces stuck in the Sambo grin

wondering how long they'll have to wait
til we take our last puff
so they can cut off our hands and eat out our hearts
as precious Black memorabilia

in a refugee camp somewhere between
Russell Simmon's mansion and Patrice Lumumba's grave
an African amputee daydreams of
American hands frozen with ice
like lice in Cecil Rhodes' hair
falling off at the wrist gangrene
calling that justice while hobbling on crutches

depraved you say
as you clutch the pearls of your privilege
and bum rush the stage
dying to become the world's richest ex-slaves.

Purely Victorious

for Ossie Davis (1917 – 2005), in memoriam

Act I

What is art
but advocacy?

(so said Ossie)

nothing created
that was ever created
was wrought
in a vacuum

all art is made in the real world
where opposites exist and collide

of rich and poor
of less and more
of beauty and gore
of ignorance and lore
of despise and adore
of ill and cure

all art takes sides

whom do you create for?
(so said Baraka via Mao and DuBois)

can't vacillate on the on the sidelines of life
while the world is backed up against the Wall Street
facing the firing squads of imperial goons
and critics
who deify dollars
and reify the status quo
with their front page lies

who don't know poverty
except as an entry in Webster's dictionary

but we who toil in the defecation of dictators
fertilize an existence from their waste
to indict and defy
those who would have us die

but with each utterance
each manifestation
of our minds
we define for all time
what we see, what we know and wish to be

the will to free or enslave
if we are conscious or depraved
is carved in the bone of our art
and we are not saved by it
whether sold or sought

what matters in the end
is the quality of our quest
for beauty and truth

all the rest
is worth no more or less
than the blood
coursing through our veins

Act II

Purlie Victorious
our whole lives are but satires
the enslaved mocking the massa
cracking up under the tracks of tears
that trek down our brown faces
we know more than we let on

sometimes
sometimes

even to ourselves

Act III

And here comes another long-distance runner

race man

carrying the baton passed on to you by Robeson
he bequeathed to you his vision and voice
and there you stood
smooth chocolate baritone

like a Mingus bass line:
(from "II B.S.")
ba doom doom doom doom
da da doimp doimp doimp
da da doom doom doom
da da doom doom doom
doom dippa doom dippa
da da da doom da da doooooooommmmmm
doimp!

a smooth bluesy
Georgia cotton drawl
spoke in the cadence of dignity
a diction of defiance
to hear you was to hear our history
calling out loud to a future yet to be to be
to be
to be
to be
true to what we know is so
a steady rhythm of words laced with longing

you constructed verse like a scientist
finding the appropriate weight or measure
you treasured words and the meanings they held

but your most precious gem
was the Ruby you wore around your heart
a courtship of commitment
your marriage was one lifelong kiss
the bliss of living on the pulse of purpose

to struggle
to fight
against those that would deny us our love

serenaded by Marian Anderson's contralto
cracking the glass ceiling of whiteness
with the siren of her sincerity

actor with the worker's heart and hands
carrying our demands to governors
who blocked the doorway to our destiny

you eulogized both King and the man you called
our Black shining prince
your words covered them like burnt incense
a holy offering
sacred incantations
that can resurrect the dead
still

your shoes cannot be filled
the soles of your feet
88 years thick
double infinity
eternity times two

who will make us live again?

who can speak words
whose truth won't choke them
before they leave their mouths?

who can utter a vision
then walk it without contradiction?

who can say with you that

"The profoundest commitment possible to a black creator in this coun-
try today – beyond all creeds, crafts, classes, and ideologies whatsoever
– is to bring before his [and her] people the scent of freedom."

I have caught a whiff
from you

Da Mayor

forever saying

"Doctor, always do the right thing."

I've got it.

I'm gone.

Whose America?

2011

A Diva Divine

for Wanda Lofton

our way is not of death
Armah's *Two Thousand Seasons*
tracks the reasons
our heartbeat is the rhythm in our music
the tempo is the ticking of time
you were never out of tune

the ancestors would say
you was an old soul from birth
wisdom pouring out from your eyes
your image made God's likeness
as sublime as Duke Ellington's "Come Sunday"
riding on his A-Train
Uptown
carrying us all the way back
through history
to show us our reflection in the River Nile

our legacy has been stolen
by the robbers of our bodies and our minds
you pointed them out to us
taught us how to see the privileged
reminding us
that the oppression still remains

your love
was as profound and real as the blues

you
you
you
Wanda
carried your divinity like a diva
like Jessye Norman singing the spirituals
your words enunciated like sonnets serenading syllables
unraveling knots locked round our minds
stopping those who would deny your humanity
and womanhood
dead in their tracks
with just one look
and a perfectly worded phrase
that would leave them puzzled for days

your ways
Wanda
were not of this world
that does not look kindly on us
you were in the church
but not of it
clearer than most are willing to admit
but we know the chasm is still here
deep as David Walker's Appeal
you carried in your bones
with the fortitude of Fannie Lou Hamer
you never stopped
directing choir from your hospital bed

there's no rest for the weary

burst into flames
speak my name you say
"I rise in fire like the phoenix"
your spirit now is everywhere

and I say
mo dupe
mo dupe
mo dupe
thank you

Wanda Lofton

for all you gave and all you give
cause I know you still working wonders
somewhere
cause you are that wonder
Wanda

and I won't be surprised
if I lift up mine eyes
on that great gettin' up morning
and see you coming back
come to find out God told Jesus
why don't you let your sistah go on ahead
instead.

A Raging Flood of Tears

after September 11, 2005, New Orleans

they are pulling our dead
out of the dead water now

they are pulling our dead
out of the dead water now

like they pulled Till out of the Tallahatchie River
and even if we did place the blame where it belongs
would they get off
like the men who murdered Emmett?

while reporters blamed us for staying
refusing to see the chains
that tied us to the catastrophe
that was to come
like when they tied Malcolm Little's dad to the tracks
and left him for dead
cause they knew the train was coming

they knew the flood was coming
they knew the levees would break
they were warned
but did nothing

they were warned
but did nothing
they refused to prepare

they are pulling our dead
out of the dead water now
counting them as if they were tallying votes
but you cannot measure disgrace with a body-count
and no one wins in death

what have we now but our heartbeats?
and tears
and the whys
of our questions keep coming

even Jesus was said
to have fed the poor
with a few fish and some bread
should we not expect more from the richest nation
in the history of the world?

scabs are being ripped away
like the homes
revealing old wounds
bleeding sores
infected by the toxic scum
of lies we ingest

as the media contrived words to describe the people
when for five days they were treated like slaves
time warped to the days of whips, chains
and names that were not our own

slave ship screams

ancestors haunt in their hollers for help
in front of cameras that don't care
sending an S.O.S. of sorrow
to a world that looks on in pity and contempt

but hope doesn't stop hunger
and faith can't quench a thirst
mouths parched in the parish
surrounded by water
but can't take a drink

yes, this is hell
the smell of rotting flesh and feces
the stench of death
like Bush's breath hot with deceit
burning under a Louisiana sun
merciless as a slave master
hysterical heat
gnashing teeth, bleeding gums
and the children
the babies delirious with grief

and still they were trapped
by the help that would come
abandoned by rescue teams on Highway 10

the help that did not help
the help that held them hostage
at convention centers that became concentration camps

no refuge
no refuge
no refuge
for the women and their children
and the elders dying in their wheel chairs

smuggled to the Super Dome
that became the prison at Abu Ghraib
blind-folded by the darkness
and tortured due to the ineptitude of officials
sinking in a cesspool of paranoia
held hostage by helplessness

how long did it take Africans
in Texas to learn that they were free?

we know how slow the government can be
when it comes to we
who are Black and poor
families again severed like before
when the auction block was swollen
with our blood and tears
the years are of no consequence

and now we wander the country
looking for wives and sons, daughters and fathers,
nanas, poppas, husbands and cousins and lovers
and friends and mothers and nieces, nephews and …
tracing the scent of love
in hope of embracing them again
on this side

pouring through web-pages
hoping to notice a name that sounds like happiness
watching the TV
hoping to recognize a face
that resembles our own
looking for family
longing for home

and I can hear Nina Simone singing
"Mississippi Goddamn Blues"
we who picked cotton there
grew families out of the very ground
we never owned
sucked down gristle just to survive
raised God out the dust bowl
and blew life into our bodies
with nothing
nothing
nothing
but the defiant desire to live
and once more nothing is all we have
but the defiant desire to live again
resurrected like the Jeez that is us

who will march a jazz dirge
on down Bourbon Street
to honor those whose bodies
still float in the 9th Ward?

who will rebuild the city
that city of saints and haints?
bring the Reconstruction that never came
after Lee surrendered the war

Jim Crow knows
let Trent Lott rot
in the rubble of his plantation mansion
for all those that perished unnecessarily

yes there is anger
a raging flood of tears

Bush looted our taxes
sent them overseas
robbed our rights
cracked presidential jokes
as the smoke still rose
"the soft bigotry of low expectations"
is Bush's to claim
a smug racism he learned on his mother's knee

yes the U.S. is a Third World nation
no corporate press can cover the truth now
where dictators lie, cheat and steal
then kill the poor that would defy them

the emperor has no clothes
his ass is exposed
been stripped naked by his own shame
time to name names

there is a raging flood
headed right to the White House

and FEMA can't rescue you now
what has happened here is a crime
the homicide of an entire city

hear the prophecy my ancestors sung

God showed Noah
by the rainbow sign
said it wont be water
but fire next time

the flames are burning!

BLOOD FOR OIL

for Ken Saro-Wiwa and MOSOP*

oil and water do not mix

so when 300,000 Ogoni marched
to protect the marshes
crying "doonu kunete" [honor the land]
the Abacha regime replied
by denying them their rights
and holding them hostage in their own homes
surrounded by the barbed-wire of pipelines
and patrolled by storm-troopers
armed to the teeth by $hell
and then they arrested you

for eight weeks you were locked in a cage
scratching defiance in the dust
while they lied on you
contrived charges
slander campaigns
but your integrity remains
rooted deep as the trees

the criminals are the capitalists
that stole the resources from the land
made knights by British royalty
while your people receive no royalties
in their crusade for crude

disease still seeds the soil
cancer grows like the grass
that once grew along the riverbank

the crickets no longer congregate there
their chorus of kora and gonge sounds
have been silenced by the fumes
that flood the atmosphere

in this war
the bullets are the very bread the children eat
live in the mouth of death

they stopped your breath
that blessed the air with conviction
you met your fate
choking at the end of rope
while your people
choke from $hell's fumes

the very ground you guarded
forced to swallow your blood
coughed up your spirit to the air
you defended

the river you tried to rescue
received your blood as sacrament
the streams are now your veins
your life lives on in the land

you who loved your artist countrymen
Wole, Chinua and Fela
but who will love you?

the leaves do
as do their trees
and the air you breathed
the water that washed you
whispers your name
in the wind
as prayer
to your people who praise you

but when the lightning strikes
and cracks the sky
in that flash
your face resides
and we hear your spirit cry

Justice!

*Movement for the Survival of the Ogoni People

Survivor

we were meant to be relished
only as mere fetish
our humanity sacrificed
to the false idols we have become
we have an identity industrial complex
they are cashing in on our confusion

unaware of how to be
we unwittingly take tips from Tonto
on how to play side-kick in our own reality
since our existence was pre-empted
so they could bring the world a new order
brought to you by Cotton, Inc.
"the fabric of our lies"

now when we speak
those are not our voices we hear
but an anglo-saxoned voice-over
like in 70's kung fu flicks
the interpreter is an interloper
manipulating what we perceive
we've been deceived
see ourselves through the bluest eyes
any wonder why
so many seek to change

          the texture of our hair
          the shape of our nose
          the color of our eyes
          our lips, hips & skin
                                        ?

pre-packaged identities
internationally shipped
complete with step-by-step assembly instructions
remote controlled de-racialized clones
2nd class versions of those
who think they are an Amazing Race
globe-trotters as narcissistic as serial killers

if only Columbus
had a camera crew
imagine what clues we'd find
to help us unbind our minds
to this master narrative

we are the survivor
stuck on a colonized island
forced to fight against each other
to win our oppressor's approval

and in the end
there is no million dollar jackpot
just a consolation prize
of being made an honorary white
a trendy transcender of thine own race
ethnically cleansed
in a society still sucking on the rind of apartheid

Dead Meat

if we are what we eat
then we are a super-sized enterprise
of burgers and fries
the globe's golden arch enemy
restaurant chains that got the land on lock
branding the earth
enticing us to jump out the fire
into their frying pan

if we are what we eat
then we are a
high fructose corn syrup sipping
sorbate sucking
guar gum chewing
monoglyceride munching
assembly line of bleached flour
being paid under the kitchen table by the hour
the world's latest wonder since sliced bread
with traveled provided by Trans Fat
"we waste no expense to rush you to your death."

if we are what we eat
then we are designer beans
high fashion caffeinated manufacturing fascists
dictating the price of trade
making deals with the IMF
to keep our stocks from slipping

star bucks who once played in the NBA
now get paid to CEOkay our agenda to the masses
who sip hot Columbians for breakfast

if we are what we eat
then we are diabetes on a stick
cancer in a cone
a stroke to go
microwaveable bowls of irritable bowel syndrome

if we are what we eat
then we are a drug-infested body politic
over-priced pill-popping dope addicts
fiending for little plastic-coated rocks
provided by corporate dealers and doctor pushers
smuggling everything from Ritalin to Viagra
across Canadian borders
pushing prescriptions
take two
three times per day
so we can stay high
from the day we are born
to the day we die

if we are what we eat
then we are less than 5% of the world's population
who devour the rest
making them refugees
who we force-feed
with blind-folded taste-tests
the entrails of our waste

telling them it's a complimentary multinational breakfast
that comes with their stay
at the all-you-can-eat buffet
where we are the diners
and they are the main entree

if we are what we eat
then we are
foul fowl
crazed cattle
spilling spoiled milk spiked with steroids
into cartons being chugged in our schools
by hormone-raging kids
with diseased mouths and feet

if we are what we eat
then we are dead meat
dead   meat
dead

                              meat

VICE-GRIP

gun shots
shell casings
and bullet shards
lodged in the heart
paramedics rush to the scene

and this is not Iraq
but Texas

seems Cheney wasn't satisfied
with sending Americans
to kill or be killed
he too wanted to get in on the action

but this draft-dodger never seen combat
except on the teleprompter
still trying to claim image of a warrior

perhaps he was pretending to be the Lone Ranger
whose mask is his own face
masquerading as human
saying HiYo Halliburton!
with Ronald Reagan's apparition riding shot gun
doing a drive-by on the whole world

or maybe he believes he is Chuck Norris
as Walker: Texas Ranger

but if he is Norris
then he is the one being noon-chucked
by an Iraqi insurgency as Bruce Lee
in "Return of the Dragon"
kicking his ass in the ruins of the American Empire

actually he's a vice-presidential fugitive
wanted by the press and the rest of the country
taking a cue from Flip Wilson
singing "loose lips sink ships"
and approval ratings

I heard he was last seen
looking in Hoover's old office at the FBI
trying to find his personal magic marker
so he can blackout the event from the country's mind
and mark it
"CLASSIFIED"

I heard a White House servant said
she saw him under the desk in the Oval Office
on the phone with the NRA on his knees
begging them please, please, please
to send down Charlton Heston from on high
so he can play holey white Moses once more
and lead him out of the sea of this bloody mess
and he promises
he'll continue to play their willing whore

we are being ruled by
drunken and illiterate white men

Elmer Fudd in a 3-piece suit
and cuff-links
wearing cowboys boots
who froth at the mouth
when they try to speak
who stutter in farts
and belch out laws
they break indiscriminately

word has it
that some men
in the Secret Service
are contemplating strike

a sign was found
plastered on the West Wing door saying:

"It's bad enough that we gotta take a bullet for the Second in
Command. But damn, we never expected to get shot by the ol'
bastard."

Deaf Jam

in Iraq
the sign language for "American"
is a hand gun.

A New Day Has Come

November 5, 2008

yesterday

i rose with the sun

and bathed myself in memories
born of blood

i reached back
and dressed myself in the whip-cracked flesh
of Fredrick Douglass

his words echoing like thunder in my head

then i put on Harriet Tubman's eyes as glasses
and viewed this day
through the far-sighted lens of herstory

when i put on my shoes
i laced up Fannie Lou Hamer's feet
tired of being sick and tired
and marched to the polls
singing her gospel symphony

when i arrived
i pulled the curtain behind me
and broke out into a breakdance

as if i were on the corner of 125th and Lenox in Harlem
reciting Malcolm X's "Ballot or the Bullet" speech

then i coughed up the shard
that shot through King
and squeezed it in my hand til it turned to dust
and tattooed the words
NEVER FORGET
on my soul

then i took my mother's hand
~ bless her heart
and together
we pulled the lever
and with millions of others
made history

and then her spirit whispered to me:

"a new day has come, son"

then i walked out of the booth
knowing that the struggle isn't over.

it has only just begun.

WHOSESALE NEGROES

Negroes for sale

they are Black
by accident

souls lobotomized
in Ivy League indoctrination camp(use)s
with PhDs in self-hatred

will proudly display
the price tag of their sell-out
dangling from their noses
long after they've been bought

lifetime members of the Strom Thurmond Honor Society

polished with wax from Ronald Reagan's ears
are ready to be placed upon ideological pedestals
as shining examples for others of their kind

more loyal than dogs
racially-neutered
and programmed to attack
whenever the word
affirmative action
is uttered by Blacks
come equipped with specially designed

brand name bootstraps
so you can rest assured they will never stray

who consider the phrase
"you're not like the others"
more than a compliment
an accomplishment

who thank God for slavery

created from the same formula
used to make the slaves
that ratted out Prosser and Vesey

they come with a lifetime guarantee
cause these negroes will die for you

who operate as a shield

consider them a steal

Whose America?

all of us did not come here on the Mayflower

/Whose America?

some of us got here against our free will
in the hulls of cargo ships
enslaved
chained to generations of sorrow

some of us were already here

/Whose America?

all of us don't live behind white picket fences
with 2.5 children
on a tree-lined suburban street
in "middle America"

some of us live in row homes
or high rises
with bars on our windows
locked down
in the projects and barrios of this nation

some of us live in trailer parks
in homes hitched to hopelessness
some of us ain't got no place to call home

/Whose America?

all of us didn't graduate from college
with a BA, MBA or PHD
to become the managers of this madness

some of us barely got through high school
where we passed through metal detectors
in class with out-dated textbooks and
computers that crash

who now take out the trash
and clean up after the mess
you've made of this world

/Whose America?

all of us are not Christians
praying to a pale-faced male god
to save us from our sins

some of us are Muslim,
Jews and Buddhists

some of us see god in the air, the rain, the trees

some of us make altars to our ancestors
and light candles to their memory

some of us believe that goodness cannot be deified

/Whose America?

all of us are not heterosexuals
trying to repress the rest

some of us are gay, lesbian or queer
some of us refuse to be bound by fear

/Whose America?

all of us are not capitalists
seeking to privatize the entire planet

some of us are socialists and communists
seeking to "live simply
so others can simply live"

/Whose America?

all of us are not white
believing this land is ours by divine right

we come in the hue of the whole of humanity
the pride we have in our people
is more than skin vanity
we remember as the poet once said,
"America never been America to me"

so we are redefining what it means to be
still fighting the Revolution
"to form a more perfect union"

marching to the sound of
Ray Charles and Jose Feliciano
singing the national anthem
their voices wrapping us in
the red, white and blues of our struggle here

no,
you may not recognize this land
when we are through

/Whose America?

"My country tis of thee …
from sea to shining sea"

watch us make it free!

THE BLACK POEM

who are we?
who we be?

standing on the corner of 125th St and Destiny
what does it mean to be Black?

cultural amnesiacs
caught at the crossroads without a map

what does it mean
Black
to be
who we be
Black

not some zip coon minstrel cartoon
Black

but true Black
Black Black
so Black
its Black as the Blues
Black

we so confused
been so abused

that we don't even know ourselves
no more
Black

our minds locked in the tell-lie-vision sets
where Black is type-cast in stereo
got us hallucinating
in horizontal lines of manufactured ignorance
seizures of consciousness
mass-marketed madness

is Black more than a color
more than a style
more than a shiny label
stuck on the back of the latest ish
a white-washed wish?

what does it mean to be Black?
was it the DJ or the DA
that turned the tables on us
left us spinning?
are we more than shiny grills
mc sambos grinning
with cavities in their craniums
Black?

platinum rims
riffin in tims

and we think we hot as hell
yet fail to see

that we the ones getting burned
at the stake
on the take
repping a Blackness that's fake
that's been raped
that's born from the minds of billionaire bigots

tell me
what does it mean to Black?

pimpin hos Black
hustler Black
ratta tat tatta gangsta Black

GOTCHA!
who shot ya Black?
but its us dying Black
now how Black is that?
is we free
Black?

when we walk around
with the word nigger
tattooed into the backside of our minds
who defines us as we is
not
knowing the truth
we become the proof
that a slave doesn't need chains
who in they right mind
would want to name themselves

after an epithet spit from the lips of those
that enslaved your great-great-grandmomma's momma?

and not recognize that we sick
we sick
we sick

tuskegee experiments: the remix
put syphilis on our souls
burned the sight out of our cipher
is we free?
see the auction block is where we live
Black
our very selves traded
still
sold to the highest bidder
can't getta job
when aint no jobs to get got

so we stuck picking cotton
outta empty lots
is this what it means to be Black
Black?
the ends justify the means
Black

you sure bout that?
cause I'm almost certain
that's just what
the slave trader told the missionary
way back in the day

how is it that we got this way
Black?

jim crow knows
but do you?

so what does it mean to be Black?

past the skin to the soul
how to get back what they stole Black
when we still being robbed

what can make us whole?
what can make us whole?

we need a new Black
Black to the Future Black
radical Black
resistance Black
fighting back Black
Black revolutionary Black

we need a revolutionary Black
we need revolutionaries Black

who will be Black
Black as Jesus Christ coming back
and save ourselves Black
?
??
???

see yourself
Black
know yourself
Black
love yourself
Black

cause the truth will set you
free
Black

When I Think of Lucille Clifton

When I think of Lucille Clifton
I think of my mother
and remember her skin
all brown with shimmers of blue sky
smooth as silk
sweet as milk
a beauty that beckons Africa
in all its fullness and sway
like the moon
like memory

When I think of Lucille Clifton
I think of my mother
her short afro just cropped
to make it her crown
and when the light hit it
just right
I swore it became her halo

When I think of Lucille Clifton
I think of my mother
a kitchen shaman
cooking up a storm
oil cracking like lightning strikes
spitting hot out the pan
where chicken thighs fry all golden crisp
as collard greens stew in crock-pots

and potatoes sit on the counter cut thick
waiting for her to mix in mayonnaise and mustard
her special brew of spices
and those deviled eggs that wouldn't last
the first go-round at the family reunion

When I think of Lucille Clifton
I think of my mother
in church
sitting in the pew all dignified
head held high
singing her hallelujahs
who knew the Bible better than the reverend
and would hold court like her Jesus
in the aisle after Sunday service
the congregation leaning on every word

When I think of Lucille Clifton
I think of my mother
a survivor's celebration
wearing her scars from surgeries
with the quiet resolve of a flower
bruised yet blooming
keloid on her skin rising like mountain cliffs
against a sunlit sky basking in her every breath

When I think of Lucille Clifton
I think of my mother
who died but did not die
whose spirit is the breeze in my memory
who stands at my bedroom door

in my dreams
smiling at her son
as he sleeps
whispering
good night.

Wife-Beater

A wife-beater is not a tank top
is not made of cotton
is not manufactured by   Hanes,
                        Fruit-of-the-Loom
                        or Perry Ellis
is not soft and comfy
does not come wrapped in plastic
cannot be bought at the local Walmart or Macy's

is not sexy

cannot be taken to the Laundromat to be cleaned

a wife-beater is not a   muscle shirt
                        an A-shirt
                        or a T-shirt without sleeves

a wife-beater is not a tank top

but does come in a variety of
                        sizes
                        and colors.

An Open Letter to President Obama

you had us from jump
on the stump
a new jack senator
searching for America's better angels
politicking in the long shadow of Lincoln

you were our brother
from another mother

we saw your wife in the reflection of our sisters' faces

we saw our children's laughter
in the rainbows of your daughters' smiles

you carried our hopes
in the throat of your measured homilies
making history in Iowa

and when they began to attack you
say you wasn't Black enough
only to say later
that you was too Black,
we watched (in the silence of our anxieties)
as you Harlem shook
the drama from your shoulders
we forgave you
when you dissed your minister

the man who married you
who taught you how to pray
only to watch them reject you still
calling you Muslim
like they were spitting on you
who enunciate your middle name
as if it were profane

we took it in stride
said it was par for the ride

but when they mocked you and your wife
on magazine covers
said you were anti-American
in league with terrorists
we were past holding our breath
sitting on the sidelines
silent
we knew we had to show our hand
we armed ourselves with ballots
aiming at Election Day

on that day
we marched to the polls
like we was marching on Selma
stood in lines that wrapped round whole townships
like we was in Soweto
chanting Mandela
we turned out in numbers never before seen
like we was Freedom singing
"Aint Gonna Let Nobody Turn Me Around"

on that night
we watched CNN
held our breath choking back disbelief
as the numbers rolled in

on that night
you walked out onto the stage with your family
Black faces beaming brilliance
Jesse's tears streamed down our faces
we achieved what no one believed
would happen in our lifetime

on that day
the heat of our hearts
pumping love
for the man about to become
the first Black prez
kept the hawk at bay
we braved Arctic winds of a DC January
just to bear witness to the history we made
with one eye on you and the other scanning the sky
we prayed
searching for gunmen with orders to snipe you
before you could take the Oath
but those days seem like a distant memory
as we gaze upon you now

when we voted for change
we didn't expect it be you

when we watched you let them perm your daughters' hair
so it wouldn't offend
some potential white voter in Ohio who dreads our locks
maybe we should've taken that as a clue
that that wasn't the only thing about to be relaxed
but we didn't expect
we'd be the ones who'd get lyed on too

what happened to the man
who conjured Kennedy and King?
who rallied millions
filled stadiums
to get a glimpse of what America could be

we knew it wasn't going to be easy
you President Obama
not King George
we get that
but that don't mean you supposed to be
the Republican's whipping boy

you pretty as Ali
but beauty is as beauty does
and we still waiting on you to rope-a-dope named Boehner

we didn't vote for you
to reach across party lines and play patty-cake
we didn't vote for you to become the muppet of millionaires
is that why you can't stand up for us?
has your spine been removed
to make room for the hand of the man

who's controlling you?
bombing the Motherland was not in the plans

we didn't vote for you
to always seek compromise
for the sake of appearances
brotherman, we see through the façade
of a government run ram shod by a lynch mob
who'd as quick set the White House on fire
and watch you burn
before they see you finish your term

joking about secession as they plot assassination

when they say
"take our country back"
they mean from you, Black
that half of you that came from Kansas don't count
as you appease the 25% that'll never vote for you
no matter what you say or do
you'll always be South Side
Chi-town
you'll always be African
without the hyphen
without the hope of ever stepping outside the chalk lines
around their minds
no matter how many millions made by your memoirs sold
you'll always be just another poor little darkie
in their eyes
your delusion
is costing us the future we fought and died for

didn't you get the memo
King left on the balcony of the Lorraine Motel
we ain't got nothing else to prove to these people
(and neither do you)

yes, yes
we know you the president of all America
but ain't we America too?

how can we pull ourselves up
when our boots been snatched
been repossessed
been foreclosed

we can't afford to live vicariously through you
in the White House
when we too busy trying to stay in our own homes

can't you see
us down here
drowning in debt
in a flood of neglect
after the hurricane of joblessness hit our doorsteps
as you fly overhead on your way to some town
where we ain't nowhere to be found

if we wanted disdain
to be ignored
treated worse than lepers
if we wanted to be dissed
we would've voted for McCain

every time we hear you speak
your breath reeks of betrayal
as you surround yourself with men
who resemble those who place our sons in cuffs
who now tell you
we can be taken for granted
that we'll always vote Blue

play us if you will
but we not the party's hand-maidens
to be treated like "The Help"
those days long gone
despite some folks' cinematized fantasies

Obama, we love you
and will always defend your right to be
the President of these United States

but we intend to hold you to these truths
self-evident
that we too are equal
and endowed by our Creator with certain unalienable rights
which we intend to pursue
with all our God-given

honestly
do you really believe
it's just the Secret Service that protects you?
that they the only reason you haven't been taken out?
don't you think they know what would happen
if you were?

don't you think they know
that we can shut this system down
overnight
and we both know they not ready for that

what I'm saying is that we got your back
have had it since before you was Commander-in-Chief
we just wondering when you gonna get ours?
gonna defend our best interests?
gonna be our ally?
gonna attack the enemies of our freedom?
gonna give us the relief we in desperate need?

who responsible for putting us back on our knees like this?
who bleeding us like this?
got us pleading like we still slaving?
what good is your America
if even after our children pledge allegiance
in schools still segregated
we can't have the fruit that falls from America's branches
watered with the blood of our family tree?

what good is you
if we still ain't free?

but even as I write this I wonder if it's too late
if you are too far gone
and we are left to our own
to bring the change you claimed

the clock is ticking
while you worry over polls and approval rates

but imagine the headlines
the day you wake up and find
a million Black folks marching on your gates.

Run

how we come to this here place and time?

primal screams
pushed out the womb into the world
by momma's love

surrounded by warm arms
laughter and smiles
… even then
there were those looking miles ahead

how we get to this place and time?

we come a long way child
and still gots a long ways to go

there were those who loved you
even before you were

those born in chains
in a land
strange

without yam and chora sounds

the drum banned
and even though they couldn't see freedom

in their dreams
they saw you

and so they endured

bodies and minds stripped
tongues slit
backs whipped

they endured

from plantation fields to factories

they endured

came home with bruised bones
swallowed insults whole

they worked hard
rubbing nickels and dimes
just to make a way
when one couldn't be seen
still they dreamed

and here you come

they worked hard
so you could study harder

and here you come

with their hope burning as light in your eyes
eager to learn

see classrooms as battlegrounds
defending the dignity of your people
passed over in textbooks

how you come to this place and time?

like morning breaks the horizon at dawn
the rest of your life lies before you

what will you do?

we got work to do
still
the world aint what it should be
still

like pastor in your grandmomma's church saying
whosoever will let them come
remake the world

see the diploma as a baton
and run runners run

run like Jesse Owens
breaking records
and racing past Hitler's racism in Nazi Germany

run runners run

remember from whence you've come
and run
run for office run
run a company run
run an organization run

we still got work to do

run

run past your fear

run

listen for the cheers of loved ones
at the finish line

run

run this relay race
ready to pass the baton on to those yet to come

and
run
run
run til the human race is

One.

Black Phoenix Uprising

2019

NAT TURNER'S BIBLE

You were not to learn the whole book
Only certain verses
Repeated like a kind of sorcery
To cast a spell on you

A book meant to make you docile
Civilize you into submission
Make you compliant with their wickedness
Teach you to obey them
As unto their god.

They hoped this would allow them
To sleep easy at night
Make you believe that the gashes on your back
Were for your own good.

They never suspected
That as they slept
You groaned in prayer
To a God that resembled theirs in name only.

How could they have known
That when you were born
Your unlettered mother read
The marks on your body
As God's fingerprints
How her spirit vexed

Found rest in the visions
She imparted to you

Was the book a gift?
Or did you liberate it
The way it liberated you?

Does it matter now
Whose blood soaked the pages
Made the verses run red
Like the words of Christ?

Even King James could not corrupt
The gospel truth
That you were meant to be no man's property.

Is it irony
That you were hung in Jerusalem, too?
Or is it prophecy?

Eternal Ally

6 Tankas for Yuri Kochiyama

1.
they stole my father.
with tongues like history books,
they lied. called him spy.
interrogated his skin
looking for signs of treason.

2.
my conviction was born
in the blast of mushroom clouds
that singed my people's souls
into the walls of my mind.
their shadows cast like statues.

3.
caged like fenced horses,
internment camp survivors
spoon-fed a diet
of model minority
rations. we refused to eat.

4.
Harlem was my home.
in her streets I found my voice.
spoke with an accent
of united activism.
liberation linguistics.

5.
Malcolm. Comrade. Friend.
killed in a gunfire hoodwink
by hired jackals.
I held his head. chaos screamed.
a red sun rising in his eyes.

6.
I am the stranger
in a homeland not my own.
eternal ally
marching for the rights of all.
I am the nail not hammered down.

Malcolm X in Africa

Black liberation envoy
bearing a passport
stamped in ancestral blood
carrying nation-building bricks
from Giza
in his briefcase

May 19, 2014
Goma, the Congo

Pretty as Freedom

for Muhammad Ali

I.

Louisville's slugger
bobbing and weaving
the jabs of Jim Crow's djinn
a prize fighter
swinging and singing
a song of wit and grit
mouth wide open
daring the world to listen in

II.

and when you changed your name
we changed ours, too
from negro to Black
no turning back
We are America
get used to us
Black. Confident. Cocky.
Our Rules. Not Yours.
Our Goals. Our Own.

Get used to us

What's Our Name,
                    Fool?

III.

And there he stood
Ali
in the center of a ring that wrapped the globe
the people's Champ as Christ
standing before the Pilate of US imperial might
in a five year title fight
bearing the armor of his skin
fists gloved in the leather of Allah's peace

he rope-a-doped a nation
proclaiming
"I am King of the World"

whose world?
our world
where we are free
to be
ourselves
Black and arrogant in our brilliance
and pretty

pretty as full bellies and clean water
pretty as a rabbi and imam praying in a liberated Palestine
pretty as reparations for slavery
paid in full
pretty as you
bearing the Olympic torch born from the bonfire
of the world's trembling desire

pretty as freedom
floating like a butterfly.

Black Fire Blazing!

for Amiri Baraka, in memoriam

in another world
you'd been president
like Senghor
Negritude's rule
Pan-Africa's promise

in another reality
you'd been prime minister
like Patrice
unassassinated by CIA soldiers

but tell the truth
and shame the devil
is what you did
cuz this be the reality
played on us
here

Baraka, they scared
still scared of you

got FBI agents
pouring through the pages of your books
with magic markers
trying to censor your memory
from our minds

as negro-fied critics lie online
make your name into a byword
in NY Times bylines
explaining how your books
never made it to the bestsellers list
as if
you sought that shit

speak the truth
shame the devil
is what you did

Black fire blazing!
Langston's raisin in the sun
an explosion of Black art against a white sky

you blew up their canon
raised a new standard
freed the verse from iambic pentameter
whose pen was a sword
taking on the National Horde
in 67
when they turned Newark into Hanoi

Leroi
we still Jonesing for you
wanna hear you pounding on the podium
as if it were a djembe
calling forth the warrior within us
cuz we are at war!
when our children's murderers

are selling their autographs
at NRA gun conventions
we are at war!
when the government been hijacked
by Wall Street terrorists
in cahoots with Supreme Court jesters
we are at war!
when our cities are ruled
by neo-colonial hustlers
corporate lackeys whose blackface is they own skin

Baraka!
we still need poems that kill
that kill ignorance
that kill apathy
that kill negrosity in cold blood

you put your verses versus the system itself
put our rage on the page
and dared the world read it
with both eyes wide open

a Marxman
looking through the cross hairs of your consciousness
taking aim

yea
they scared
still scared
and now respectable afrodemics
with alphabets after they slave names

locked in ivory towers
wanna shower you with fake praise
talk about freedom of speech
let them do a phdeed study
on why your skull got cracked
let them dissertate on the affirmative action
of your knocked-out teeths
they are but double-dutched men
dodging bullets on NY subways
trying to convince bernard goetz
they not like the rest of us

but you
juju master of the Black Arts
left them on pins and needles
voodoo wordsmith
casting spells on the ill
                              -iterate
cracking the shell of European syntax

there was no shuffle in your walk
no stutter in your talk
no bougie in your boogie down
and got down you did
for the workers
the peasants
the wage slaves
for them that get they labor depraved

you will forever be
Poet Laureate of the Proletariat

you said
it's not enough to write
the poem
the play
when we don't control the stage
and the whole world is a production
ownership of means
by any means
by any means
by any means
necessary

you
a synthesis
of Malcolm and Mao
a dialectics of defiance
from Marx to Monk
a blue funk
as avant-garde as Tubman
going back to the South with nuttin butta shotgun
talking way out
where you is now
       wayyyyyy
       out
on the surreal side

that owl exploding is you now
in the tree of life
eyes big as Baldwin's
with Malcolm X-ray vision
seeing thru they bullllllllllllllllllllllllllll shit

like Coltrane's horn blowing our minds
forever who who-ing
asking the questions where most fear to tread
naw you aint dead
the lecturer lives on in us
who still here
sippin from your stream of consciousness

raise the Black nation worldwide!

we forever call your name
that sounds like thunder
clapping in standing ovation

BARAKA!
BARAKA!
BARAKA!

Free the Land

for Chokwe Lumumba

revolution is the acquisition of power
by any means

you were our means necessary

Mississippi bluesman
New Afrikan
marching out of Michigan
with a Motown rhythm in your step
repping the one once known as Detroit Red who said
"The Ballot or The Bullet"

you the manifestation of Malcolm's analysis
consciousness cocked and ready
aiming at City Hall
a tall blade from the grassroots
with New Afrika's promise
rising from the horizon of your eyes

speak the truth
like Cabral
you told no lies
claimed no easy victories
when our liberation remains the prize

                    not a tv show
                    or a blockbuster movie
                    or an academy award
Chokwe in the land of the Choctaw
when you took the surname of Pan-Africa's Prime Minister
we should've peeped your endgame then
you came to liberate a city
named for a presidential enslaver

in the land that lynched little Emmett
whose swamps swallowed civil rights workers whole
spied on SNCC
and denied Fannie Lou a seat at the DNC convention
Mississippi
where Myrlie watched them murder Medgar
in their driveway

Goddamn!
how our blood cries from this land
you knew
the struggle is protracted
staring down our detractors
sniffing out provocateurs

where is the Black nation?
what is our analysis?
our plan?

what are we to do
when our children's blood runs cold
in these streets?

when their schools fail
to teach them the truth
producing minds dilapidated as our homes?
what are we to do
when the prisons are swollen with our millions?
rusting away like the corroded bars
that got them on lock

Who rules the block?
really
when the homes of corporations scrape the sky
lining the pockets of those we put in the power seat
while we are left scraping just to get by

but you were
incorruptible
a will forged of granite
special as we all are
each of us
when we decide to do right

and though we may never know
how or why you died

we know you live on in us
in our Black proletariat aspirations
for you are now our North Star
the highest light that cast no shade
Kujichagulia's constellation
guiding us to Freedomland
to Free the Land

to Free this Land

and when we say
Free the Land
let us mean it in the same way you did
not to merely rhetoricize
but to realize
what we need here and now
to love the people, the land
the life that feeds us
nurtures us
gives us the strength
 to fight on

when we say
Free the Land

let it be in full consciousness stride
like them that freedom ride
who decide to boycott the back of the bus
who risk life and limb to win us free
from the chain, from the sharecropper's claim

Chokwe Lumumba!
for true
and when we have freed the land
we will rename the City of Jackson
after you.

Blacklisted at Birth

Langston Hughes before the House Un-American
Activities Committee

Are you now or ever have you been
a member of the Communist Party?
they asked
and asked again
of the most famous Black poet in the world
from Kansas
in an America before Brown vs. Board of Ed

summoned to Congress
to give a kind of command performance
by politicians who made the laws
that made his citizenship into a mocking cynicism

interrogated by the very men that schooled Hitler
them that spoke fluent Nazi
Lieber tot als rot
a slight paraphrase of the old American proverb
"the only good nigger is a dead nigger"

was it swastikas he saw circling in their irises?
or were the whites of their eyes enough
to clarify their intent?

hellbent as they were
to make him recant his work
to renounce the Renaissance he helped wrought
from his brownstone in Harlem
an interrogation that became
some kind of extraordinary rendition
choke back his words or face social death

surely he was must've recalled how they revoked
the passport of his friend a few years before

Did he then wonder if he'd need to go into hiding
like Neruda did when they outlawed communism
in Chile in 1948?

Maybe he saw them
bash in his head and knock out his teeth
and arrest him for inciting a riot via a poem
like they would do to a later poet in 1967 Newark

Or perhaps he saw them cutting off his fingers
and laughing as he bled
like Pinochet did to the poet Victor Jara in 1972
before assassinating him in front of a stadium of thousands
that would share his fate

But then he must've seen the pictures of the
Africans who sat beside their severed hands
in shock

on rubber plantations
punitive damages for not bringing in the daily yield
in King Leopold's Congo

were these workers communists too?

but this poet was made to suffer through
these unintelligent interrogators
frisking his verses for signs of treason
as they butchered his words
to make the claim that they lacked
the appropriate measure of patriotism

he knew there was no explaining his work to men
who had no appreciation for the varieties of speech
of similes or subtleties of discourse
of irony or hyperbole
not to mention satire

for them language was a blunt force
used only to bark commands
and bludgeon judgments

dumbfounded as they were to understand
why a Black man
would ever consider another economic system
better than the one
that placed his grandmother in chains
sold his pa down the river

and keeps him working in the same fields
under threat of lynching
while telling him that he's free

did they really think he needed some Russian to tell him
that being called a boy was not a term of endearment
when his poetry had already made the point?
for him
America was all but a bloody stubborn metaphor
he knew that he and his people
were capitalism's necessary curse

there was no need to be concerned for being red-baited
when he was already blacklisted at birth.

They Will Kill You

for Trayvon Martin

they will kill you and say I'm sorry
and expect your mother to forgive and forget
she ever gave birth to you
carried you in love for nine months
endured labor
and pushed you out
with God's might moving in her hips
ever fed you life from her bosom
or how you smelled like heaven
after she washed you
that she ever watched you
take your first steps
speak your first words
ever tucking you into bed
with stories that rocked you to sleep
the many nights she prayed for your protection
or how excited she was the day you gave your first recital
that she ever taught you to be good and kind
ever beamed with pride
whenever you got an A on your test
that she ever wanted the best in this world for you

they will kill you and say I'm sorry
and expect your father to forgive and forget
ever holding your tiny body in his hands
for the first time

and looking into your eyes and seeing eternity
ever teaching you how to ride a bike
or the many nights he helped you do your homework
how he worked hard to make your life easier
or playing catch with you in the backyard
or the life-lessons he recited to you
over the rhythm of hair clippers
ever scolding you with stern words and reassuring hugs
ever kissing your cheeks
or how he was there week after week
cheering you on from the stands
how he dreamed that you'd graduate high school
go to college
fall in love
and that he ever wanted this world to love you too

they will say I am sorry
and expect your mother and father to forgive and forget
the day they learned of your fate
when the ground collapsed beneath them
and the earth swallowed their hopes and tears
as it did your blood

they will kill you
and say I am sorry
and expect your mother and father to forgive and forget
that you ever existed
that you ever existed
they will shoot you
and pin you down in the pool of your own blood
suffocate you in the torture of your screams

and watch you die
they will leave you rotting in the morgue
as your parents lose sleep and hair
wondering where you are
on a trip down the block
to buy some skittles and iced tea

they will douse your memory
in the gas of gossip
and burn your body in the effigy
of lies and race hate

they will tie you to blog posts
and whip your image
til it is twisted and distorted
unrecognizable to the ones who loved you first

they will kill you
and raise money from the dead body
that was you

they will kill you and expect us
to forgive and forget.

As if we were a town in Tulsa

for Terence Crutcher

Bullets cracking bone spilling blood
Of bodies crashing into asphalt
As deputized cowboys stand around
Share high-fives in earshot of our dying gasps
Curdling through bloodied coughs
As our lungs and life collapse

And still we are made to stand
Hand over hearts
Propped up by bayonets of their militia men
Wearing tri-pointed hats singing Yankee songs
Scribed by men who celebrated our slavery

Yet we are not meant to make connections
Meant not to remember past yesterday
To ponder the known and the unknown
Ourselves

Instead
We are supposed to recite a script
Written in textbooks printed in Texas
That teach us that we were immigrants

Swimming across the Atlantic
To work for free in this melting pot called America
When we are the ones being burned

As if we were a town in Tulsa

Conspiracies

for Sandra Bland

They would have us think
You took your own life
In that dank cell
Where cameras failed to work
That night

They would want us to entertain
The possibility that the cop
Had probable cause
To pull you over that day

They want us to trust them
When they told us that was you
Alive
In your mugshot

They would have us accept
That you were suicidally depressed
Even after landing a new job
That you were headed to
That day

They would have us not question the coroner
Because she is a Black woman
Like you
Like us

They would leave us
Wringing our hands in wasted frustration
At witnessing another injustice yet again
On a roadside in Texas

And when we still insist that they killed you
They will call us conspiracy theorists

There was a young woman on her way to the market in Mali
When she was stopped by men bearing guns
She never made it home that day
Her body would be found in a holding cell
As the salt water of the Atlantic lapped its dank walls
No mugshots
No orange jumpsuits
No phone calls to her family
All that is left of her life
Is the evidence of her name changed
In the scribbled dialect of a captain's log
On a ship from Europe
As cargo

Our whole lives
Have been the unraveling of a conspiracy
That was done to us
On those shores
What we know
Is that there will never be enough evidence
To justify our existence to them
Or our right to one

There will always be
Some catch
Some clause
Some law
Or some before unknown hidden something
That will be used to silence us
To stop us dead in our tracks

From those who never ever have to
So much as blink a worry
Of a traffic stop being
The beginning
Of the end
Of their lives.

Godly Transgressions

for Ce Ce McDonald

Most Christians be quick to say
"God works in mysterious ways"
but can't seem to see
the Divine
at work in you.

Psalms for Palestine

Netanyahu,
your flag may bear the star of David
but the Palestinian people bear his spirit;
twirling freedom's slingshot
hurling the bleeding stones
of their defiance
in the face
of your iron-clad Goliath.

Elements

four haiku for Sonia Sanchez

Fire

she freedom's passion
plantations burn in her wake
fearless as Tubman

Water

her words water our hearts
cleansing our consciousness in
salt-water soul baths

Earth

poems jump borders
you contraband joy laughing
a world's resistance

Air

the cosmos ululating
a new world breathes within you
dawning jubilee

A Love Raging

for Colin Kaepernick

it didn't matter that you got the idea to kneel
from an army vet

we had our hands up high as goal posts
saying "Don't Shoot"
but that didn't arrest their bloodlust
didn't cease their fire

when you took a knee
you took your place in history
beside Rosa Parks and Ali

playing a position
still the preserve for white men
but you are nobody's Brady
conducting interviews
with the likeness of Malcolm and Fidel
emblazoned on your chest
as if it were a crest of arms

replying to each question
with the nerve of Angela
eyes alight with a truth
they can't contain
can't ascertain
taking on an entire nation in a denial

as old as itself
suffering from a concussion of conscience
since those pilgrims first hit Plymouth Rock

and they have killed to keep it that way

but we know this

What you endorse is no longer dictated by Wall Street stocks
you represent the people without voice,
without choice
the mothers screaming into the void of an ever-waking nightmare
fathers seething in sorrow
whole hoods up in the flames

you carry a world circling on an axis of pain
on shoulders tatted with wings
our arch angel carrying a message
from the nether world
where our dead congregate still waiting for justice served
their names hashtagged into our memory

with one silent act
you spoke louder than a riot
a love raging against a blue wall of violence

Hail Mary

a segregated country club of white men
bearing a title that is a throwback
to when the fields Black men worked were called plantations
no coaches but overseers paid to keep them in line
with a referee's whistle of whips splicing the air

for them
owning the team
means
owning you too.

first branded by the NCAA
you were the poster boy for college recruiters
marketed to rich white kids
seeking that real college experience
complete with frat parties and binge drinking
and you were still poor, labor unpaid
sold a hope that one day
you will play in the national football league

seasoned by millionaire coaches
to ask how high when told to jump

we know
they care more about your knees and ankles than you
to them you are a kind of property
bought and paid for on a national auction block

called the draft
by teams of white execs who have never played a down
but are given the gentleman's bargain
to scrutinize your body and abilities
with the thoroughness of slave traders.

Let's be honest here.

Could they care any less
that one of us killed could be
your brother, your sister, your own son or wife
or you, Black
or you?

as if you ain't got no relations with us no more.

OJ you into thinking you are beyond race
a class unto yourself.

But we remember you
young boy running ball
first downs marked by car lengths parked on
narrow potholed streets.

we remember you
carrying your team to the state championships
coming home to celebrations where momma's cooking
was on full spread
as one and all
lovingly chided you to mind those grades

so you could get that full-ride
praying that trouble wouldn't find you
but trouble is all we know
and we in real trouble now.

with this move they've shown their hand
and the discrimination of its complexion

we can no longer pretend
that this is just a game

our lives are on the line
and yours is too.

What we know
is that
there is no game without you.
No new stadiums to fill.
No billions to be made.
No anthems to be played.
without you.

Luke Cage

skin thick as Harlem brownstone bricks lit
in neon crucifix
a Blaxploitation flick on steroids

a Romare Bearden collage riffin in Tims
conjuring Jack Johnson
an unforgiveable sin

Tuskegee experiments remixed in shades of melanin
a hoodoo totem protection
a blessing and a curse

bulletproof Blackness
a white cop's nightmare

the dream of men with barb-wired halos
land-locked in ships of steel

the living embodiment of a Black power fist
marching down Malcolm X Blvd
in broad daylight

Black Phoenix Uprising

They call us magic
when it's just us being who we are
scarred and black

We resilient as sunrays
no way to comprehend it
so we name it as God

Yet
we are the holy without the ghost
the evidence of things unseen
the spirit within us has no need to haunt

Black vortex of the inexplicable
the word made flesh
enchantments of the divine

We speak in tongues
native and colonized
still conjure the force of creation
like volcanoes erupting
we enunciate new worlds into being
and name them all freedom

Ancient as the pyramids
When we congregate
we come together not just to remember
but to resurrect the dead

We the progeny of those that dared be free
who been to hell and came back
smiling through bloodied teeth

Black phoenix uprising

We are an insurrection of fire
reborn from the bone embers of our ancestors
a righteous indignation igniting revolt
in the minds of the assassinated
dynamite exploding from our mouths
heat hollering past hotness
burning like the north star

Though some of us were once
tarred and feathered
we been known to fly
our wings span centuries

Talk to me of love
personified
of a million Black souls reincarnated
into the backbones of our sons and daughters
their freedom dreams etched into our genes
forged from centuries of revolt
a cauldron of liquid fire

poured like a shaman's rum into these charmed skins
epidermis of steel
melaninated mutations
trauma alchemized to genius

Our badassness been long archived
no need for every episode to be televised
our revolution be satellite beamed from our eyes
bright as liberation yearning
smoldering a beauty that would leave the world blind

We are root connected by the sodder of Ogun
beating life from his blacksmith's hammer
on the anvil of our hearts conjoined
bleeding like lava
no matter where in this world
our blackness is common cause
is kin that goes deeper than this skin
mood vicarious
maybe that's the reason
we often cry without knowing why
or when we deja vu in blue
every step taken in kind
this the collective conscious of the wretched
the damnation of the yet vexed

Whatever justice there is in this world
comes from the kerosene flame burning within us
comes from our conviction
like the match that strikes
the match that lights

the match that ignites
our will to remake this world
like we remake ourselves

African again

before the English, the Spanish,
the Dutch, the German, the French
and the Portuguese

before we were chained in those ships
before Leo Africanus
when what we knew ourselves to be
was the genesis of humanity
that indigenous spark
that will remake this world

They say we are magic
but that is just us being ourselves
scarred and black
we resilient as the sun rising
no way to comprehend it
so we name it God.

New/Uncollected

2014-2023

Trumped

from the backwoods of American history
comes a white riot marching in folds of pig's skin

a spoiled brat turned robber baron
bamboozling Appalachian workers
seeking to collect dividends on their psychological wage

Capitalism's Freudian slip
The Grand Id of Imperialism
Napoleon Bonafart with a complex to match
the ass of the ruling class
a tax-dodging sociopath,
flag-waving fascist
marching to the echo
in the cave of his small mind
who can't speak in intelligible sentences
without the aid of a teleprompter

Internet Troll-in-Chief
commanding millions of minions
hanging on his every tweet

who has all the civility of a serial rapist

an ass backwards bigot
whose speech is a hate crime
conferring with klansmen and conspiracy theorists

whose preferred greeting is a Nazi salute
who would turn the Secret Service into the SS

a constitutional conman
whose campaign was a shell-game
elected in a democracy that's never been
whose term is an impeachment in process
backed by the same financial interests
as the 3rd World dictators
that are responsible for his government training

the Great White Dope
the 4th Stooge
A celebrity TV Scrooge
the Devil's Apprentice
whose love is the root of all evil

consider this white supremacy's last dying gasp
and whatever label given is but a warning
who is a more imminent threat to humanity
than global warming

The Only Medicine Necessary

for Fannie Lou Hamer

there was no mistaking your voice
running deep like Mississippi waters
flooding the streets King and 'em marched in
moaning night revivals
seeking salvation from the terror of segregation
and the death threats that kept your phone off the hook

daughter of sharecroppers
picking cotton before you were old enough to know why

yet there was nothing servile or submissive about you
your singing was more than melody
it was an eruption of antebellum ring shouts
bellowing from a world even them that marched didn't know
liberating hallelujahs from back country church benches
to Democratic party conventions

and after they beat you
with the puppeteered hands of men
who shared your skin and caste
with guns to their heads
as white cops beat you in your face
who could have blamed you
had you turned bitter as the taste of blood
clotting in your mouth

or cold as the walls locking you in
or hardened as your bruised body swollen was made

instead your heart got larger
wide as your mouth open in song
like an Akan in triumph

Mrs. Hamer
we are still taking beatings
they are still shooting us
still warehousing us in prisons
robbing us
still being turned away at the polls
and stealing our votes
still exploiting our labor
keeping us disenfranchised
want to put us back on those plantations

teach us how to fight
how to carry the weight of this troubled world
as divine yoke
teach us to see the light thru this darkness
to see ourselves as you do
as worthy of the rights we take for granted
of the wealth we create for others
of the homes we are not allowed to own
of the churches they bomb, burn and shoot us in
teach us how to love
when all we know is hate
how to love right and not white
show us with those hands

wrangled from all the cotton you picked
how you dip that love into tubs of indigo
and hang it dry
so it can be hugged by the wind
and kissed by sunlight
then wear it like the royalty we are
teach us how to hold our heads high
like you did
and not just act all dignified
but be dignity personified.

let us hear you
loud and uncompromising
in the righteousness of your song
you the summer rain in freedom's dawn

sick and tired of being sick and tired
your love
the only medicine
for all that ever will ail us

Apocalypse Rot

"Imperialism leaves germs of rot
which we must clinically detect
and remove from our land
but from our minds as well."
Frantz Fanon

Who knew the apocalypse would come by way of cough?
that a sneeze could kill you
like a scene from The Walking Dead
"avoid each other like the plague"
is no longer cliché

What we fear is the dread our lives always been
unmasked now for the matrix of lies
unplugged
as we huddle in an insanity of isolation
inhaling the hot toxic phlegm of a fool
masquerading as commander-in-chief
stockpiling toilet tissue
but can't wipe away the shit stain of disgrace
from his clown face
whose make-up is an artificial tan
and colored wig is his own hair
or so he'd have us believe

Thinking he could somehow ban a virus at the border
treat it like it was some Muslim immigrant
or detain it like it was the child of Mexican parents

listen to the way he says China
enunciating his bigotry before the world

Yet it would seem this virus votes Republican
preying as it does on those with pre-existing conditions
as though it were a double agent
for some right-wing conspiracy
concocted by pharmaceutical lobbyists on K Street
trying to espionage the cure from Cuban doctors

Could it be that the ones calling this a war
are the ones that fired the first shot?
who failed to provide coverage
cut the budget to the CDC
leaving our loved ones to rot in make-shift morgues
dignity robbed as final rites denied
can't touch
can't say goodbye
no final baptism in the palms of our tears
a mass grave dug by their laissez-faire disregard
for our humanity

America's sins are the death wages now paid
to those made to survive
on the bare minimum

How many lies have we been told
by those that would have us replace
the Rod of Asclepius for the dollar sign?
who would sacrifice their elders
to save an economy that never saved us a nickel or a dime

let alone our lives
and we are still expected to pay rent

"And this too shall pass"
doesn't account for those that have passed
doesn't account for those left to mourn them
quarantined in a quagmire of misery
unless we are diseased of heart
cold and corroded as the senators
who vote down relief packages
ignoring their own test results
kept immune to the pain of their constituents

and yes
we are dying
we are dying
we are dying
we
are
dying

In Europe's dark ages
they believed
you cast out demons when you sneezed
which is why we say God bless you
yet our prayers can't stop the dying
or bring them back
tell me how did it come to this?

Preachers too busy proselytizing prosperity scams
to read the signs in the heavens

claiming healing for those that send in their tithes on time
via online cash apps

And all this did was reveal
the wounds on the body politic
the immorality of unsolicited touches
garbled speeches and gaffes
by presidential hopefuls
an unrepressed racism
rabid as mangy feral dogs
diseased by a dementia-ed democracy
on life-support

It would seem that the Earth itself has cursed us
suffering from a seasonal flu that never ceases
a perennial fever raging in storms,
earthquakes and tornadoes
whose only cure is the doomsday of a species
who've shown themselves to be the actual virus
now put in a global time-out

And we are running out of time
time is running out
for us who walk on two feet,
speak, have opposable thumbs and cover our loins

Our enemy is not nature
but those that have designs to wrap in plastic
and put on their shelves
and sell to us what is already ours to share

What would the dead say to us?
except that we need to change
yet if not for them,
then for ourselves most certainly for the children

Let them know a world without words like
trafficking, exploitation, extraction,
fossil fuel, minimum wage

Where a free market is where you go to get groceries
not the stocks that keep you in bondage

Let them know a world where health care is free
as the air we breathe
and let the air become our friend again

We must envision a new way
believing what we know
that a new world is not just possible
it is essential
if we are to survive

So now we're calling all dreamers to the front-lines

All the poets, singers, painters and seers
all the upstarts and agitators
those unsettled with the rot gut
known as the way things are
the socialized rut we rat race in

Vision us a new world
rendered by the needs of bees
as vast as the trek of polar bears wanderlust
measured by the memory of elephants
and the rise of the oceans on the coastlines
as urgent as the fires raging in Australia

A vision indomitable
as the aboriginal peoples
that have everything to teach us about this world

While the sun still rises in the East.

One Drop Placebo

for Harriet A. Washington
for Dr. Bill Jenkins
for Dr. Susan Moore

Ours is not some putrid concoction of deceptions
contrived by a confederacy of hucksters

Our fret is not with science per se

We know full well
what's been done to us in its name
by those enrobed in white

How we've been frankensteined
in the laboratories of madmen
who measured our skulls after killing us
said we were soulless as they savaged us

Whose eureka came from rape
and boiled tortures in glass beakers

Our blood measured in quadroon one-drop segregations

Babies lab ratted by doctors
whose names grace university halls

Our black hides stretched under government microscopes
bodies laced with disease
like the blankets you gave the Shawnee

Do you really expect us to forget Tuskegee?

You lied to them
hundreds of men
told them they were being treated
as you prescribed pills coated in contempt
so you could watch them suffer
jotting down notes with the disdain of judges
signing death warrants

And you wonder why we don't trust

Seeing one of us get shot in the arm cheesing
ain't gonna change none of that

Did we miss the memo?

Missed when you paid damages
and signed acts as acknowledgment of injustices
injected in doses of desuetude
as more than apologies emptied
of the actuals to address what ails us

When what ails us most is you?

But that would be too much like right
too much like reparations

How is it that laws meant to protect when applied to us
have the same effect as a placebo?

When doctors are known to ignore our pain
leave us wasting in hallways
gasping for basic dignity
send us home even when we are doctors like them
then claim us hostile as prognosis
as though we should suffer peacefully
die gracefully
like when we get shot in these streets
and left to rot for hours as roadkill

When the walls next door got more rights than our Black lives

Since when you care
whether we live or die

Since when?

Too Black Too Strong

for Malcolm X

You were
our Blackness reinvented
by the necessary of our condition

A pride chiseled in your flesh

Defiant as a mountain
and as abrasive

You put the diss in dissonance
a sonic boom clash of dissent
bombarding our senses with an incessant chant
of right and exact
a pariah to those ensconced
in a status born of our bloodshed

Your voice cracking the mirror of their God complex
your disposition was ever vexxed
held their head fast to the truth
with the threat of drowning them
in your stream of Black consciousness

You called their bluff
dropped aural bombs
obliterating their self-proclaimed bombast

Your voice an alarm resounding
waking us up from integration fantasies
as fraudulent
as ploy and entrapment
designed to keep us in check
serving up assimilated wishes on platters of respectability
suffering from a psychosis of the infirmed
hemorrhaging under a hundred years hegemony of self-hate
your homilies reverberating with the rhythm of a djembe

What we know now
is what we've always known
your assassination was an american gestapo
a cabal of FBI informants in cahoots with the NYPD
they conspired to kill you
your murderers making deals
on who would take the rap and who would walk
the main gunman living out his life under the arches of a mosque
portrayed as a saint who was a killer
hidden in plain sight
literally lived on the film that recorded your death
as your body rushed across the street
to the hospital where you would be pronounced dead
the very man pretending to resuscitate you
was an agent pretending to be a Black man
like the man now ruling the city
where you once held court
a cop called mayor
wearing the camouflage of his skin
bamboozled his people to win the office
who wants to bring back stop and frisk

These are the times we are living in

Times you prophesied would come to a people
still being led astray
conditioned to measure justice
by how much a family gets paid
when our children are murdered by police

Is this some sordid civil rights severance pay
for cops who continue to terminate our children?

Or is this some sort of reparations for a people still unfree?

Or are we again being hoodwinked
by race hustlers who know how to talk the talk
but stutter in their step?
For them marching is a media stunt

Degreed negroes making cream
Signing mega deals with media conglomerates
while victims' families still catching shit

A class of house negroes
left in charge of the plantation
who'd have us live vicariously through
their acclaim and success
while we remain without a defense
singing we shall overcome
someday

As governors post tip lines
for white parents to snitch on those
who would dare teach openly about the likes of you
our history as education
as passport to the future

These are the times we are living in

History is stuck on repeat
as a regime foments civil war
with crosses on their tongues burning

They have always known of our power
that's why they take such lengths to control
to distract us with negroness
and bourgeoisie carrot sticks to chase
while they sit in the stands and place bets
on those who will lose
when we are the race, the track and the runners
on our backs they've saddled up

Yet some of us still study you
your life
follow your steps from Lansing to Boston
to prison to Harlem
to Mecca to Ghana
to London barred at France
and back home to a family firebombed

These are the times we are living in

Where the world's majority is brewing in a sea of rebellion
leaning on your every word
undeterred like your smile
broad and bodacious
winking with a foreknowledge of our rising

Righteous as the truth made plain
righteous as the return of ill-gotten gains
righteous as your voice
an eternal echo in the chambers of our collective mind
booming like a Public Enemy soundtrack
reminding us to always be

Too Black Too Strong
Too Black Too Strong

COME CORRECT

My countenance is a steady brood
Like Richard Allen at the city's edge
Contemplating the freedom of a race
Exorcising demons from the dispossessed
Erecting sanctuaries with his DNA engraved in its stone

Deep into this present darkness peering
Into a horror that even the mind of Poe couldn't scope

Lurching in the shadow of the first gentrifier
Looking over a city long lost
Where death is legislated by a class
Of compradors whose descendants claim
Eminent domain of a history stuck on repeat
Squatters on the land of the Lenape
The great con that stole a continent
And left them frozen in statues of noble
As saxoned savagery is let loose in Schulkylls of blood

Their progeny mummering down Broad Street
In blackface as projectile parody on those their prey
Rizzoing

I live in the long shadow
Cast at high noon
The wild wild western civilization
Always Outlawed and Wanted

Ever targeted by minutemen
Wearing the tricorn hats of hitmen
Pirates profiling as patriots of a Nation
Born in the blood of my kin
Who would napalm this country
Before see it run by jawns like me
Yet our seeds are watered by fires bombed on our homes

My body runs electric
Copper veins channeling frequencies of soulforce
Charting rivers of blood
From an ocean
Where history set sail
And condemned the world
To a catastrophe

I am
The consequence of conquest
A phobia spawned from the minds of enslavers

Look into the black of my irises
Surrounded by a sea of white and see
Ten million souls screaming
Divine wrath coiled as my nerves
Convulsing in this temple

My every utterance is an oath sworn
To those
Trapped and bound in tenement hells
Drowning below deck
I am the resuscitation of their saltwater memories

And Here I Stand
In these streets echoing ancestry
Consider this a forward or a forewarning
If you step to me
Come correct.

Jesus in Texas

for the children massacred in Uvalde, May 24, 2022

Jesus hangs on a cross in Texas
suspended above two nations

His body a mangle of bullets

the men who sell the guns
don't speak His native tongue

they cast lots beneath Him
for the land His tatara abuelo once called home
before it was stolen by desperados

His mother is alone
crying at His feet
Her tears handcuffed by a history
that denies Hers

preachers mispronounce His name
slapping his face
in a mockery of prayers

in a nation unrepentant
where no salvation is found
by those who worship in the torment of His bloodshed.

Why I Write

I write to fight

My words a raging torrent
against this present torment

I write
Cuz this love can't be caged or tamed or renamed

When I write I go hard
like Jacob wrestling that angel to gain his birthrite
I write to fight for what and who's mine

No presidential Hancock hypocrisy
inks the parchment of my soul
My constitution is signed by those they chained
and like those that escaped
I leave it all on the page

I write for every law that made it a crime
for us to learn how to read
My writing is a centuries old clapback
Revenge screed

For every whip mark
For every mutiny
For every white man
who made specially sized chains to fits babies' hands

For every noose tied around our necks
Every slave ship
Every cross burned
Every rape
Every gun shot

For every hashtagged memorial
For every Black life that didn't matter
For every time they burned their names in our backsides
For every scrape
For every bow
For every not yet or never now
For every time they called us uppity
And the times they tarred us, scarred us, mucked and mired us
For every time we were denied
For all the lies they taught us in their history books
I write to set our truth free

For each and every time we had
to swallow ours to survive
For every smile that masked our anguish
For every child forced to walk
through a storm of white hysteria raining rocks and epithets
on their way to school
For those that refused to give up their seat

I write cause I don't have no other choice
like fire shut up in my bones
scraping graffitied manifestos across the sky
how I stay lit
blessing the mic with offerings to the Ancient Ones

not for profit
less we talking about Old Testament poets and scribes
rationed on a diet of wild honey and locusts

Wise as madness
in a world where sense is not common
and the rule of law is oppression

Call me possessed
but I say I'm just a vessel of flesh
blessed to be tormented by the cries of those lost,
never to be found
those middle passage drowned and the downpressed now

My breath is but the whisper of their every defiance

I write to create sanctuary from the hell
we know here
cause the world is already on fire

I write to record
every dream we each have ever had
and those to come

For the drum
that beats life inside my chest of bones

For Gwendolyn, Mari and June
cause Baraka taught me
Haki and Askia too

Because Sonia told me to resist
and so I do

I write for the God in me
I write for the God I see
when we come together to organize for our right to be
ourselves
Black and True

I write to spark the flame in you.

Fahrenheit 1492

A Contraband Poem
A Critical Race Poem

> *"Colonialism is not satisfied merely with holding*
> *people in its grip and emptying the native's brain*
> *of all form and content. By a kind of perverted logic,*
> *it turns to the past of the people and distorts,*
> *disfigures and destroys it."*
> **Frantz Fanon**

for real though
it's kind of understandable
when you think about it

I mean who would want their history such as yours taught?

when you consider what the record actually says
as recorded by your own writers, philosophers
(if you can call them that)
who created the idea of race

trace the contours of history and what do we see?
except it written by killers, conquistadors and enslavers
men who called themselves white
as right
as to say superior
men who never would've imagined
that the people they put in chains

would ever be able to one day
read their captain's logs let alone their diaries

but here we are

with the legacy of shame in today's terms
laid out plain

so yea
we get it

given your history of violence
such as it is ...
each page bleeding
with the guts of peoples from every corner of the globe
pilloried in the name of your privilege denied

would take a magic marker to your history
and mark it classified like the FBI
to hide all the dirt you've done

want the whole world
like you
uncouth to the truth

as if we ain't living that history now
you don't want them to know about Emmett Till
or thousands of Black people lynched
cause they might make the connection to
Trayvon Martin
Michael Brown

Sandra Bland
Breonna Taylor
Philando Castille
and all the others unnamed
and come to you reeling from the sense of betrayal

yea I guess it makes sense
for someone as weak-minded and fragile as you

but what you trying to do
ain't nothing new
our history been black-marketed since
you outlawed us learning
caught lashes on our back or worse
if caught with a book in hand
or when we stole ourselves free
from your plantations
as contraband
and crossed enemy lines during the war
that you still deny
you fought to keep us enslaved

this is your brain on white supremacy
the disdain is palpable
it would be laughable
if it weren't true
got guns to the heads of teachers
daring them to tell the truth

ban books written by us
cause it hurts your brains

to read what terrible human beings
your fathers and mothers were and are

don't want your kids to see granny
spitting rabid at little Ruby Bridges
or the owner of America's team
smiling as his friends beat
Black kids integrating lunch counters in the South

you were good when all the books were written by you

whited out
Frederick Douglass,
Nat Turner
and Sojourner Truth,
Ida B. Wells
you lie about Pocahontas
but erase Geronimo,
Sitting Bull
and Tecumseh
made mascots out of those you massacred

Colonized Puerto Rico,
Hawaii,
Guam,
Haiti,
Alaska,
the Philippines

Elvis Presleyed history

teach Thanksgiving
and tell us
the Indigenous just gave up their land
and walked onto reservations
willingly

published textbooks in Texas
teach we got in those ships ourselves
the chains were decorations
happy smiling darkies
"The Help"
not slaves
just "unpaid"
we volunteered our lives away
the whips were for our own good
like why you got us locked up in these hoods

or like when you banned the Chinese
from these shores
said they were like vermin
as in spreaders of disease
just like you tried to do after Covid-19

you would have us believe that the West
was just one long John Wayne movie

some of you cool with us learning about concentration camps
in Germany
not the ones here
that interned Japanese Americans for being Japanese
said it was national security

like you do now with those who pray to the East

ever uneased by Identities you can't police
who live outside the confines you've manufactured
during your Dark Ages

your beauty standards are ugly
as you looking back at yourself in the mirror of time
ugly as the horror you unleash

why
who's the only who
to drop a nuclear bomb on another country?

and you wonder why you ain't well-liked

consider that
just about every world problem
began with a decision made by you
for the sake of brevity
we'll begin in 1492

who said white was so special?
that the rest of the world should worship you
as God?
sent missionaries around the world
to demonize our way of life
called us savages as you savaged our lands

when you teach your children to pray
you want them to imagine God as Santa Claus

who loves all the world that he gave his only son, begotten
not as the rotgut burner of women at the stake
not as the namesake blessed on the side of slave ships
not as the crucifiers of the Taino
who cut their babies in two
to test the sharpness of their blades.

what we realize is that
there is no metaphor
more descriptive than you
in all your actual horror and filth

so what will you do?
burn books?
or burn the people you don't want writing them?
a fascist's decision, right?
but we not supposed to be that bright
not here in America
and yet here we are
where fascism is as racism does

you see
when we called it a theory
that was just us playing nice

the fact is
ain't nothing theoretical
about what has gone down

the fact is
there is no telling our story

without revealing you
as humanity's constant antagonist

the fact is
you can't handle the truth

the fact is we yawn at
your every pronouncement
of freedom and justice
as farcical
which is to say that
nobody believes that madness
except you

we see you for what you are

gaslight the whole world
and if that don't work
you'd set it on fire and
burn it out of spite

yours is a meritocracy of mediocrity

can't stand to see Black people happy
and you have the nerve to call us dysfunctional
how many Black men been lynched
or murdered by cops
on account of a white woman
raised to lie with tears weaponized?
it is this very inheritance of arrogance
a blood privilege

passed down in willed estates of callousness
a sense of entitlement tied back
to family discussions and friendly bets
on who'll get to own the next pickaninny
(that's what you called our children, right?)
born on the plantation

this for you is about more than books
it's about banning our lives
rendering us unread by the world
judged by the cover of our skins

yet we are the text and testament
words walking in these tenements and barrios
each sacred as the next

we long done ripped ourselves
from your paper-thin script
the false narratives of your false consciousness
now unbound
we don't subscribe to your borders
live our lives beyond the pale
of your laws and legislation
giving perpetual side-eye to your sorry-ass ways

our truths, tis of We
are evidenced by every author
you despise and devise to ban
we been ever wise to you
as in hip

or woke
after all, we come from the people
who said
every shut eye ain't sleep

but peep this
even when we couldn't read or write your words
we read you up and down
with a slow gaze of knowing
older than you

you, who'd have us believe a lie
a lie as white and foul as your beliefs
as your violence wrapped in the coda of law
as your ignorance masquerading as value

every lie you have ever told
has come back in your face
as your own disgrace

how does it feel to be rendered naked
before the world
as a fraud?

call it white supremacy
when there's nothing supreme about you
at all

Biographical Note

Ewuare X. Osayande was born in Camden, NJ in 1970. He has published twelve books of poetry, essays, and speeches. His last book of poems, *Black Phoenix Uprising*, was published by Africa World Press in 2020. His other books of poetry include *An Afrikan Awakening* (1993), *Caught at the Crossroads Without a Map* (1999), *Blood Luxury* with an introduction by Amiri Baraka (2006), and *Whose America?* with an introduction by Haki R. Madhubuti (2011). In his introduction, Madhubuti, founder of Third World Press, writes, Osayande "is a story-teller not defined by zip code, but as the best poets have done and do, he claims the earth and its peoples as his subjects. His voice is singular, urgent and a drumbeat redefining a world of possibilities for all." His books of essays and speeches include *Black Anti-Ballistic Missives: Speeches Against War and Racism* (2003), *Misogyny and the Emcee: Sex, Race and Hip Hop* (2008), *Commemorating King: Speeches Honoring the Civil Rights Movement* (2014). Osayande's poetry is included in a number of anthologies including *Black Fire This Time* (2022), and *What Lies Beneath: Katrina, Race and the State of the Nation* (2007).

Osayande is a former adjunct professor of African American Studies at Rutgers University-Camden. From 1999 to 2002 he served as the chairperson of the Philadelphia chapter of the Black Radical Congress. In April 2005 Osayande was the first poet to have a symposium on his body of work at The Institute for the Study of Race and Social Thought, Temple University. He is the 2006 recipient of the Walt Whitman Arts Center's Vanguard Writer's Award. In 2014, he edited the global anthology *Stand Our Ground: Poems for Trayvon Martin and Marissa Alexander*. "Protest and Politics in the Work of Ewuare Osayande" is a graduate course taught by Dr. Joyce A. Joyce at Temple University. Osayande is the founding editor of The Poetariat, an international journal of social justice poetry.